JIM CROW'S PINK SLIP

SERIES | RACE AND EDUCATION

Series edited by H. Richard Milner IV

OTHER BOOKS IN THIS SERIES

Urban Preparation
Chezare A. Warren

Justice on Both Sides
Maisha T. Winn

Truth Without Tears
Carolyn R. Hodges and Olga Welch

Millennial Teachers of Color
Edited by Mary E. Dilworth

Culturally Responsive School Leadership
Muhammad Khalifa

Science in the City
Bryan A. Brown

Race, Sports, and Education
John N. Singer

Start Where You Are, But Don't Stay There, Second Edition
H. Richard Milner IV

The Chicana/o/x Dream
Gilberto Q. Conchas and Nancy Acevedo

Restorative Justice in Education
Maisha T. Winn and Lawrence T. Winn

Teachers of Color Resisting Racism and Reclaiming Education
Rita Kohli

Stuck Improving
Decoteau J. Irby

JIM CROW'S PINK SLIP

THE UNTOLD STORY OF BLACK PRINCIPAL AND TEACHER LEADERSHIP

LESLIE T. FENWICK

HARVARD EDUCATION PRESS
Cambridge, MA

Paperback ISBN 978-1-68253-719-0

Library of Congress Cataloging-in-Publication Data is on file.

Published by Harvard Education Press,
an imprint of the Harvard Education Publishing Group
Harvard Education Press
8 Story Street
Cambridge, MA 02138

Cover Design: Ciano Design
Cover Image: Daniel Kaesler/EyeEm via Getty Images

The typefaces in this book are Minion Pro and Myriad Pro

This book is lovingly dedicated to my extraordinary and inspiring parents and my remarkable husband.

For teaching me the art of writing, I thank my mother, Mrs. Glenda Faye Ward Fenwick.

For modeling deep knowledge and appreciation of Black history, I thank my father, Dr. Joseph Wyeth Fenwick III.

For Herculean support and indispensable wisdom, I am grateful to my husband, H. Patrick Swygert.

CONTENTS

FOREWORD

TO DATE, the Race and Education Series of the Harvard Education Press has examined, in my view, some of the most pressing issues in education. Studying and advancing knowledge about race, racism, and racial justice remain essential to the work of educational researchers, policymakers, practitioners, and community members. The series has focused on curriculum, instructional, assessment, and relational practices. Moreover, drawing from their rich and robust research, experiences, and practices, authors have written about a range of other topics and issues. They have offered empirically based recommendations that have contributed to classroom-level discourses as well as national debates about race. Authors in the series have studied practices, preferences, and experiences of young people, educators (including teachers and school leaders), as well as policies and structures that shape people's learning and development. I hope the series has made a difference for researchers and theorists. And I remain optimistic that the series has been a gamechanger for practitioners and policymakers. But most importantly, I believe the series has been and will continue to be a tool in the movement for equity and justice with, for, and through young people.

Leslie Fenwick's book, *Jim Crow's Pink Slip: The Untold Story of Black Principal and Teacher Leadership*, joins the important scholarship in the series with a must-read book about our nation's failure to truly fulfill *Brown* because we abandoned the mandate to integrate Black principals and teachers into desegregating schools. To be clear, although the series has made significant contributions to scholarship on racial justice in education, Fenwick's book breaks new ground in several significant ways. To my knowledge, *Jim Crow's Pink Slip* is one of the first books to provide a historical analysis of the purposeful and largest purge of educator talent ever experienced in the US public school system. The book chronicles how and why the illegal transfer of educator jobs from Black people to white people after the *Brown v. Board of Education* decision crippled Black leadership of public schools and ultimately stymied the nation's progress toward educational equity.

Using the 1971 Hearings before the Select Committee on Equal Educational Opportunity of the US Senate on the Displacement and Present Status of Black Principals testimony as its point of departure, this book examines how from 1954 through the 1970s, nearly one hundred thousand exceptionally credentialed Black principals and teachers across the seventeen dual-system states were systematically and illegal removed and replaced by less-qualified white educators. Fenwick meticulously and powerfully documents the mechanisms created and used by state legislators, school officials, and locally elected leaders to resist integration of Black principals and teachers into desegregating schools. *Jim Crow's Pink Slip* ignites a new understanding about school desegregation and concludes with a series of recommendations aimed at diversifying the nation's educator workforce and redefining school reform and transformation.

The book represents the very best of what it means to learn from history to inform and understand current day issues, perspectives, policies, and practices.

In this powerful analytic merging of history, policy and practice, Fenwick engages issues of race, whiteness, and privilege (and as subtext, may make a case for reparations) as she conceptualizes how structures and systems have been developed to maintain segregation and an inequitable status quo. She invites readers to learn about what has precipitated and sustained a troubling teacher (and pedagogical) and principal (and leadership) pipeline. In this way, her critiques and insights situate the historical, amplify voices of Black educators, and delicately propel conversations about justice and equity policy and practice.

Drawing from an established body of scholarship and her own deep and robust analyses, Fenwick uncovers important connections between desegregation efforts and the current underrepresentation of teachers and leaders in schools. Indeed, Fenwick invites readers to ask: "What implications does [history] have for modern day public schools, Black student achievement, education policy formulation, and diversity in the educator workforce (specifically, teaching and school leadership)?" Thus, this is not only a book about history and desegregation. This is a book about the importance of history in our journey to deepen our knowledge to inform our practices about current day educational efforts for justice and diversity.

Jim Crow's Pink Slip offers much. Perhaps most importantly, drawing from a deep and wide empirical database, Fenwick demonstrates how Black educators were exceptionally educated—well prepared to teach in segregated and desegregated schools. In this sense, Fenwick's work disrupts the lie that Black educators were somehow "feebly" qualified to teach and lead. To the contrary, as Fenwick details, Black educators had developed knowledge, skills and capacities (through both traditional credentialing mechanisms as well as nontraditional ones) that often far exceeded those of their white counterparts. A transformative tool for those experienced and newer to education, this book adds an essential layer to the storyline about the reach and influence of Black educators, pre- and post-*Brown*.

Every educator, scholar, practitioner, community member, and policymaker concerned about racial justice inside and outside of education should read this book! This book teaches as it truth-tells.

—H. Richard Milner IV
Cornelius Vanderbilt Distinguished Professor of Education
Vanderbilt University

PREFACE

I STILL REMEMBER THAT DAY. It was sunny and cold. Irritated by what I thought was a deficient lecture on the politics of education, after class I marched from Ramseyer Hall to Ackerman Library on a mission. My mind wasn't racing. It was dragging with the same, persistent, wearisome internal dialogue I'd had with myself since elementary school. "I'm tired of this!" I thought. "For God's sake, I'm a PhD student, and this is *still* happening! With all the abundant research resources on this campus, my professor can only conceive of Blacks through a lens of pathology and deficit?!"

This professor was typical, not an outlier. Well-meaning as he believed himself to be, he had begun his opening lecture with a roster of statistics. You know the drill: Blacks are 80 percent of this and 90 percent of that.[1] The *this* and *that* were all bad. I remember raising my hand and asking the professor if he thought that by providing naked statistics (without any history or framing), he was reinforcing racist notions about Blacks. It seemed to me that of all places where discussion about the impact of the social-political-economic order would take place, a politics of education course would be among the foremost. At the time, I didn't know (and neither did the professor) that my question was a (very loose) paraphrasing of W. E. B. Du Bois in his study called the *Philadelphia Negro*. "A slum is not a simple fact, it is a *symptom*," Du Bois wrote. "To know the removable causes of the Negro slums of Philadelphia requires a study that takes one far beyond the slum districts."[2] Du Bois's scholarship forcefully situated and balanced the Black condition in a worldwide context (note his next book, *Africa and the World*) and within America's racially oppressive and capitalist frameworks.

The first three chapters of Du Bois's *Philadelphia Negro* are devoted, in his words, to "a study of the family, of property, and of organizations of all sorts. It also takes up such phenomena of social maladjustment and individual depravity as crime, pauperism, and alcoholism."[3] Clearly, Du Bois did not barter away examining the functional in the Black community to focus exclusively on the dysfunctional (or behaviors that may be described as responsive to apartheid American society at the time).

Rather than my query to the professor leading to a deep Socratic teaching moment, there was utter silence in this classroom of PhD students. Stiff. Necked. Utter. Silence. And it was that utter silence which hung to me on my march to Ackerman Library. For once and for all, I was going to end this incessant assault on the truth about Black people.

During my childhood schooling, I thought the misrepresentation of Blacks was an oversight by White teachers unfamiliar with the detailed lessons on Black history that I had learned at home from my parents. But that day, as a doctoral student, I concluded that these teaching acts that haunted my classrooms were either evidence of woeful or purposeful miseducation. The perpetrators were culpable and inculpable, captured by and perpetuating their own miseducation and socialization, which were thoroughly embedded with consistent lies reifying Black pathology and inferiority.

In his 1997 book *Black Art and Culture in the 20th Century*, Richard Powell makes a statement about the misrepresentation of Blacks in art that I believe has relevance to the portrayal of Blacks in research. "These images took the form of outrageous characterizations of Blacks, their communities, and their alleged cultural practices," Powell observed. "These grotesque beings were usually shown in impoverished settings with yard fowl, watermelons, and so on. Alternately backward, shiftless, ridiculous, childish, criminal, these characterizations faithfully appeared in . . . theatrical productions, popular literature, advertisements, children's toys and other cultural documenta."[4]

The scholarly research community has much to learn from Black artists about "imaging" Blacks. Early Black artists and photographers used their art to lay claim to a position alongside, and yet distinguishable from, accepted categories of the great and the beautiful. For instance, the February 2012 issue of the *American Art Review* describes the work of the artist William Edouard Scott (1884–1964) as follows: "[He] created paintings and murals throughout his life that focused on elevating the stature of African Americans. Generating artwork from Paris, Mexico, Haiti, and the American South, as well as Indiana, his artwork frequently interpreted Blacks in positions of prominence, a bold and uncommon approach for his time. He rejected the conventional portrayal of African Americans as menial laborers or historical enslaved persons."[5]

The imagery of Scott and Black artists of the Harlem Renaissance demanded that Black painters and photographers refute theories of Negro inferiority and display the bonds of affection and community among Blacks that were rarely acknowledged by White media. Black artists and writers led the way in creating a collective image of Blackness that launched Blacks and their voices into the realm of American public life. By contrast, the contemporary scholarly community has not yet crafted a new renaissance moment.

To be clear, a disproportionate share of Black scholarship (especially in the social sciences) has been devoted to correcting the record by critically reinterpreting history and debunking racist ideations and outright neglect in the research literature. James D. Anderson best critiques this miscasting of Blacks in research literature in his award-winning 1988 book, *The Education of Blacks in the South, 1860–1935*, where he defeats the oft-repeated sociological conclusion that Blacks really do not place a premium on educational attainment:

> Thus, it is ironic that in time a body of historical and social science literature was built up which tended to interpret Blacks' relatively lower levels of educational attainment in the twentieth century as a product of initial differences in attitude or cultural orientation toward learning and self-improvement. [However,] a careful examination of Blacks' enduring beliefs in education and their historic struggle to acquire decent educational opportunities against almost overwhelming odds leaves little room to attribute their relatively low levels of educational attainment to uncongenial cultural values or educational norms. That more was not achieved means little, for the conditions have been appallingly difficult.[6]

Were it not for Black scholars confronting profoundly entrenched (nearly concretized) mythical histories about the Black condition, the myths would remain and inure to the benefit of ignorance (and racial hostilities, misguided policy, and funding interventions). These myths are especially prevalent regarding the traditional history told about the *Brown v. Board of Education of Topeka* legal decision, which established that racial segregation of children in public schools was unconstitutional and harmful to the development of children, both Black and White. The traditional accounts, as Vanessa Siddle Walker and Ulysses Byas explain in *Hello Professor: A Black Principal and Professional Leadership in the Segregated South*, "reduced all Black schools to unilateral inferiority because of inadequate facilities," while more recent histories "invite new dimensions into the traditional story."[7] These newer histories constitute a myth-breaking, an unmuting and telling of omitted facts and narratives that seek to show what actually happened and how things were in pre-*Brown* segregated Black schools.

Here I must return to that cold afternoon march to Ackerman Library, where I sought data to share with my professor to refute his negative assertions about Blacks. Instead, I happened upon (quite by accident) transcripts from the June 14, 1971, *Hearings before the Select Committee on Equal Educational Opportunity of the US Senate on the Displacement and Present Status of Black School Principals in Desegregating School Districts*. Since their publication, these transcripts have been cited in numerous books and scholarly articles about the tragic firings and demotions that befell Black teachers and principals during desegregation. Many scholars reference the transcripts in their striking descriptions of Black principals and teachers as critical community leaders and civil rights actors.[8] With a few exceptions, the seminal research on Black principal and teacher displacement has focused exclusively on segregation-era Black teachers, not principals, presenting the teachers as community uplifters, activist leaders, and tireless foot soldiers "who [bred] dissatisfaction with and opposition to racial discrimination" as they pursued education for the "Black masses with religious zeal."[9]

Previous research has examined the collective fate of Black principals and teachers, but only in a few states or specific school districts. In 2004, Linda Tillman produced a comprehensive analysis and bibliographic summary about Black principals pre- and post-*Brown*.[10]

Though the existing research literature consistently cites the 1971 Senate hearings on displacement of Black principals, none of it presents and deeply analyzes the transcripts' most predominant and compelling fact: that the Black principals and teachers who were illegally demoted, dismissed, and fired as a result of White resistance to *Brown* almost always possessed academic credentials and professional experiences that exceeded those of their White peers and those who replaced them. Since the early 1900s, in fact, significant numbers of Black principals and teachers had, through a confluence of circumstances, earned master's and doctoral degrees from some of the nation's most prestigious universities—Columbia University, the University of Chicago, the University of Pennsylvania, the University of Michigan, New York University, and Iowa State University, to name a few. The 1971 Senate hearing transcripts presented state-by-state reports showing that the displaced Black principals and teachers also held higher-level professional certificates and showed higher rates of certification than their White peers and those who replaced them.

Alongside the story of the displacement of this highly credentialed Black workforce is the remarkable and little known history of Black educators who, forced out of their own states by segregation, went on to earn doctoral degrees from nationally prestigious universities such as Harvard University, the University of Chicago, and the University of Pennsylvania in the 1920s.

This 1920s intellectual revolution among Black educators was in large measure (though not exclusively) led by Charles Thompson, the first Black person to earn a PhD in educational psychology from the University of Chicago (in 1925). In addition to being a compatriot of W. E. B. Du Bois (the first Black person to earn a PhD from Harvard, in 1895), Thompson served as dean of the Howard University Department of Education and, in 1932, founded *The Journal of Negro Education* (JNE). JNE is the oldest continuously published, refereed scholarly journal on issues incident to Blacks throughout the diaspora. Thompson served as a collaborator with Charles Hamilton Houston, Thurgood Marshall, and James Nabrit, the attorneys who crafted *Brown*, and he used JNE to document the condition of Black schools and colleges, explore the implications of segregation, and promote desegregation efforts led by the NAACP and other civil rights organizations. Thompson conceived of JNE as a vehicle for disseminating rigorous research aimed at eradicating racism and segregation. He and others purposely crafted an intellectual agenda that resulted in Blacks gaining academic credentials and social experiences at nationally prominent universities, which they then used strategically to go about the work of improving the academic heft of Black segregated schools in the South.

For three important reasons, the *1971 Hearings before the Select Committee on Equal Education Opportunity of the U.S. Senate on the Displacement and Present Status of Black Principals* is the primary resource informing this book. First, the more than one thousand pages of hearing transcripts and supporting documents (state reports, *amicus* briefs, interviews and personal testimonies, letters to state and federal officials, and civil and human rights reports from the field) are the most comprehensive and robust evidentiary support about the annihilation of the careers of Black principals and teachers. The hearings are especially important because the personal testimonies and interviews were delivered by an array of individuals (some under oath) directly affected by Black educator displacement and/or supportive of their cause, including Black principals and teachers, government officials, civil rights attorneys, university researchers, and executive directors of professional associations.

The Senate hearings represent, first of all, a "pinning down of as much textual evidence" in the "words and works of the people" who lived this history—including both those who were affected by the atrocities described and those perpetuating the acts.[11] *Jim Crow's Pink Slip* seeks to reflect what is said about the historians' responsibility: to "teach us a variety of ways to read the past."[12] This story seeks to present an unconsidered perspective about Black educators with the hope that a constructive tension is created with the telling of this history that moves forward our assumptions, inquiry, and conclusions about Black educators prior to and during the *Brown* era.[13] Using document analysis and historical policy analysis (the latter, primarily viewed through the lens of relevant court cases), this book reflects a certain notion about history and myth-breaking: "History is a science in collecting, finding, penetrating; it is an art because it recreates and portrays that which it has found and recognized. Other sciences are satisfied simply with recording what has been found; history requires the ability to recreate."[14]

Jim Crow's Pink Slip is another recreating of the story of *Brown* with the intention of forwarding knowledge and a shift in popular sentiment about Black educational excellence, the results of *Brown*, and the quest for a public school system that reflects democratic values.

Second, contained in the hearings are the state-by-state reports, legal briefs, research studies, newspaper articles, and investigative reports from the Black press and White news organs, as well as opinion-editorial articles examining the causes of Black principal and teacher displacement. The nationwide effort to collect and present these reams of data and reports before Congress was led by the National Association for the Advancement of Colored People (NAACP), Black educators, and the state affiliates of the American Teachers Association (ATA—a professional association of Black teachers and faculty in segregated Black schools and historically Black colleges/universities); civil and human rights organizations such as the American Friends Service Committee (AFSC); and largely White professional associations such as the National Association of Secondary School Principals (NASSP), the American Federation of Teachers (AFT), and the National Education Association (NEA)—all of which were firsthand witnesses to how desegregation was unfolding in the southern states. Remarkably, as early as 1918, AFT had called for equal pay for African American teachers, the election of African Americans to local school boards, and equal educational opportunity for Black children. This interracial collaboration of organizations to ferret out the truth about what was happening to Black principals and teachers represented a powerful counterpoint to the protracted and often violent White resistance to the *Brown* decision.

Third, the Senate hearing records of personal testimonies, *amicus* briefs, and especially the court cases make it clear that the firings, demotions, and displacements of Black principals and teachers were happening in purposeful and chronological lockstep and that resolution was needed to stop the loss of both. In short, decimation of the ranks of Black educators should not be viewed separately, but as a whole cloth, given the similar tactics used against and the resulting fates of Black principals and teachers in the dual-system states.

Due to their comprehensiveness, the Senate hearings are essential to the twofold purpose this work, which is (1) to tell the untold story of how Blacks strategized to gain exceptional academic credentials in an effort to transform segregated all-Black schools into spaces with intellectual heft; and (2) to upend the often-repeated myth that *Brown* ushered in newly found freedom for Blacks, which led to their abandonment of public school principalships and teaching positions in favor of new and greener employment pastures. Too much research and commentary has erroneously reached this ahistorical conclusion.

Sadly, too, the lie perpetuated by segregationists of the era to keep Black principals and teachers out of desegregating schools has made it into the research literature about *Brown*, as illustrated by an egregious assumption and assertion that most Black teachers were feebly qualified. To the contrary, in 1952, 72 percent of Black teachers were college graduates—an almost 40 percent increase since 1940 and a figure within a few percentage points of White teachers.[15] In fact, in a 1965 study, *White and Non-White Teachers in the United States*, the NEA found that 85 percent of non-White teachers held a college degree, compared with only 75 percent of White teachers.[16]

In the literature that reflects this perspective (a perspective proven inaccurate by the 1971 Senate hearing records), there is little to no mention that, despite the injustices and stigma inflicted, Black people constructed a strategy and exercised leadership to make their schools' academic programs superior to Whites'; the primary method of achieving this goal was to build schools populated by exceptionally trained principals and teachers. For instance, in an obscure history of science achievement at all-Black Sumner High School in Kansas City, Kansas, prior to *Brown*, Manheim reports on a resounding theme of this book, the exceptional qualifications of Black educators in segregated Black schools. "In 1939," he writes, "44 percent of Sumner's teachers had master's degrees, and by the late 1950s, there were several PhDs at Sumner and Lincoln [the other Black high school]. Conversely, in White schools of the time, teachers rarely had more than bachelor's degree."[17]

In the dominant mythistories, Black principals and teachers who were discarded along with Black schools were inferior and shabby relics of a Jim Crow era. But what does it mean to recognize that these displaced Black educators were, in fact, superior in their academic credentials, professional licensure, attitudinal commitment to democratic ideals, consistent activism against the ideology of racism, and experience with integrated society?

Yes, it is true that Black schools in the South suffered as a result of resource deprivation, and yes, Black principals and teachers managed with what was available, in many cases succeeding against the odds. But let's be clear: the overarching goal of integration was to give principals, teachers, and students the full opportunities that only an open and integrated America could provide.

Jim Crow's Pink Slip's focus on displaced Black educators' credentials is essential, because these credentials stand as evidence against the ubiquitous lie of Black intellectual inferiority. Rather than confirming Black incapacity, these educators' credentials affirm their equality (and superiority) and self-agency. Their credentials affirm their determination not to be stymied by all the odds stacked against them in the Jim Crow South, and to maneuver this evil system to their and their communities' uplift and advantage. Emphasis on this essential fact makes this account historical and truth-telling in a way that other accounts about Black educators to date have suppressed or ignored.

This book is not an analysis of *Brown* or its implementation. Nor is it a panegyric to segregated schools and a romanticizing of Black principals and teachers. Rather, it is the first book to tell the untold story of two generations of Black educators who, beginning in the early 1900s, accelerated their education credentialing, became the nation's most qualified group of educators, and built schools (literally and figuratively) that nourished Black students, only to be captured by the arc of racism, summarily discarded by the nation's public school systems, and replaced by less-qualified Whites.

I still wonder how and why the prolific citations of the Senate hearings—which from beginning to end focus almost exclusively on the exceptional credentials of displaced Black educators—have not been subject to detailed presentation or analysis in the hundreds of subsequent narratives and books about desegregation. It is as if the segregationists' assertions about Black schools and the professionals who inhabited them have been substantiated—without evidence, or in direct contradiction to the evidence—in the research literature and commentary about *Brown*.

Black principals and teachers of this era were not simply warm nurturers fondly captured in the loving memories of their students (though there are ample accounts of this warmth). This book about Black principals and teachers presents a different story—that of Black educators who were powerful models of intellectual authority and who sought, fought for, and gained exceptional academic credentials as part of their personal and communal fight for unfettered equality and full citizenship in American society. Their fight was against a life and future abridged by the ubiquitous insult that they, as Blacks, were intellectually or in any other way inferior. Their story is exemplified by leaders such as William A. Robinson, who in 1913, after earning a bachelor's degree at Atlanta University, a historically Black college/university (HBCU), went on to earn a master's degree from Columbia University in 1924 and to serve as president of ATA. As a teacher, principal, and state supervisor in segregated Black schools in Washington, DC, Tennessee, Georgia, and North Carolina, Robinson advocated for a progressive education and earned national prominence for his work to expand high school education for Blacks in North Carolina.

Robinson was not the only one of his kind; there were many, many Black women and men like him serving as principals and teachers in segregated Black schools. In fact, Robinson was more the rule than the exception. While there may be stories here and there about an individual Black educational leader who is an exemplar, the collective history of the many "Robinsons" who led Black segregated schools is too often overlooked or unknown. This is their story: the story of a collective who used education to push against the oppressive arc of "race madness" and second-class citizenship.[18]

The history, research, and commentary about Black people is plagued by what I call the *theory of cultural elision*, which I define as an operative lens leading to the purposeful disregard, unseeing, and incomprehension of anything positive, self-determinative, or superior about Blacks. In the telling of history, the conducting of research, and the phrasing of social commentary, application of this operative lens results in valorizing White males and promoting Whiteness as normative and positive. To the contrary, anything positive or superlative about Blacks is reflexively left out—as if it simply could not be so. In most leading research, histories, and commentaries about Blacks, Blacks are seen as striving toward a White ideal and high mark. If, on the odd chance, Black excellence is acknowledged, it is usually tied to a single Black who is then exceptionalized in the research, history, and commentary.

In recent years, this theory of cultural elision played out in news stories about US President Barack Obama's appointment to the *Harvard Law Review* during his days as a law student there. News accounts exceptionalized Obama for this achievement. To be sure, Obama was the first Black president of the *Review* and had served as one of the editors in years prior. However, the telling of his ascension to the *Review's* presidency led many in the press to conclude, erroneously, that there had been no Black male editors of the *Review* prior to Obama. In fact, the first Black member of the *Review* was Charles Hamilton Houston, who served as an editor in 1921. (Incidentally, that same year, Jasper A. Atkins became the first Black elected to the *Yale Law Review*). Houston was a graduate of the all-Black Paul Lawrence Dunbar High School in Washington, DC, and a Phi Beta Kappa graduate of Amherst College, where he was valedictorian of his class. He earned his law degree *cum laude* from Harvard University in 1923. Houston was followed by two other Black editors of the *Review*—William Henry Hastie and William T. Coleman. Hastie was also a Dunbar graduate and Phi Beta Kappa and *magna cum laude* graduate of Amherst College; he served on the *Harvard Law Review* in 1930 and earned his Harvard Law degree in 1933. Similarly, William T. Coleman was a *summa cum laude* and Phi Beta Kappa graduate of the University of Pennsylvania who was first in his class at Harvard Law School in 1946.

Ultimately, the purpose of *Jim Crow's Pink Slip* is to rewire the telling of the history of desegregation by focusing on the exceptionally credentialed generation of Black educators who were purged from public schools in southern and border states during decades of White resistance to the *Brown* decision. I situate this story in the time period directly before *Brown* and through the administration of US President Richard Nixon. This story links the history of *Brown*, the rise of Black educational leadership, and its subsequent (orchestrated) demise after *Brown*. This book seeks to answer the following questions: Who were the fired, dismissed, and displaced Black principals and teachers (by name and circumstance)? How did they become more credentialed than their White peers, especially during the early- to mid-1900s, an era of constricted and legalized racial oppression? Why and how were Black principals and teachers purged from desegregating public schools, how did they fight back, and what were the outcomes of their battles? What implications does this history have for modern-day public schools and diversity in the educator workforce (specifically, in teaching and school leadership)?

In telling this story, I seek to challenge the quaint notions about Black educators of this era. In fact, these principals and teachers were prized by their students because they were learned, intellectual powerhouses who, as a group, understood the science of teaching and learning—because of their exceptional training—in ways their White educational counterparts did not. They necessarily maintained high standards in their teaching, served as mentors to their students modeling a commitment to democratic values and anti-racism, and equipped those students with strategies to fight the discrimination they would encounter when they went into the world, because these educators had fought and were continuing to fight the same fight.

The expulsion of Black principals and teachers was not exclusively a loss to Blacks and the South; it represented the most significant brain drain from the US public education system that the nation has ever seen. It was so pervasive and destabilizing that, even a half-century later, the nation's public schools still have not recovered.

1

WHO SHALL LEAD?

It was quite all right to have Black [principals] for Black kids in Black schools, but if the schools were to become centers for the education of all children regardless of race . . . naturally Whites would be in charge.

—National Association of Secondary School Principals report, 1971, reporting on the recalcitrant view of southern officials about desegregation

In a war, there must be some casualties, and perhaps the Black [educators] will be the casualties in the fight for equal education of Black students.

—US Department of Health, Education, and Welfare report, 1970

What is happening is not integration; rather it is disintegration—the near total disintegration of Black authority in every area of the system of public education.

—National Education Association report, 1970

THERE IS AN IMAGE our minds conjure when we hear the words, "1954," "*Brown versus Board of Education*," "desegregation," and "busing." Etched in the national memory is the stark black-and-white photograph of Black children gazing straight ahead walking through snarling White mobs toward a schoolhouse door. We think of the South—Alabama, Mississippi, Georgia. We think of South Boston, too.

BROWN IS NOT ANCIENT HISTORY

What may be more important is what we fail to consider—what we *don't* think about. First, the drive to desegregate schools is not ancient history.

Though the famous *Brown* decisions came down in 1954 and 1955, desegregation did not occur in many school districts until 1968 and well into the 1970s. Second, while the nation's schoolchildren today represent diverse populations, the educator workforce is not similarly diverse. The lack of Black educators, in particular, has a history associated with the implementation of *Brown*. In the early 1970s, White resistance to the Supreme Court decree decimated the Black principal and teacher pipeline and intentionally resulted in massive demotions and dismissals of exceptionally credentialed Black educators. As Black student enrollment grew in the nation's desegregating schools, the numbers of Black principals and teachers fell dramatically. In contrast, White educator appointments thrived, even as White student enrollment declined in desegregated schools (due to White flight). As school desegregation slowly played out over the decades since *Brown*, White principals and teachers became its direct beneficiaries, while Black educators were its primary prey.

Nearly 40 percent of public school students in the US today are Black or Hispanic/Latino. Almost 10 percent of the nation's schoolchildren are English language learners (ELL) who speak a first language other than English. Half of ELL students are born in the United States. Adding to this mix are urban settings where schools have 90 or more nationalities represented in their student body. In these schools, "Black" can mean Somali, African American, Nigerian, or Jamaican. "Asian" might mean Japanese, Laotian American, Pakistani, or Vietnamese. Hispanic/Latino might mean Dominican, Mexican American, or Honduran. In these twenty-first-century schools, the word "White" hides shades of difference, too. Are we speaking of an Uzbekistani immigrant, a White American of Italian descent, or a Jewish American?

This multicultural collage does not exist, however, in the ranks of those who lead and teach in the nation's schools. There is a tremendous demographic mismatch between the nation's public-school personnel and the student population it serves. Approximately 7 percent of the nation's teachers are African American. Nationally, 91 percent of teachers in urban settings are White. In inner-city schools, 73 percent of teachers are White.

Among the nation's principals, roughly 11 percent are African American.[1] Notably, 65 percent of principals in urban schools having predominantly African American and other minority student populations are White.[2] Fewer than 3 percent of the nation's nearly fourteen thousand school districts are led by African American superintendents. This is so even though the nation's most academically credentialed and professionally experienced educators are Black.[3]

Unfortunately, a national mythology operates about why the number of Black educators is so dismally low. The myth goes like this: with desegregation, Blacks left careers as public school principals and teachers to pursue professions previously restricted to them and more financially lucrative. The truth is quite different. Massive White resistance to the *Brown v. Topeka Board of Education* decision (the 1954 Supreme Court decree that ended segregation in public schools) prompted the firings, demotions, and dismissals of legions of highly credentialed and effective Black principals and teachers. The fight to decimate the ranks of Black educators was so pervasive and severe that its fallout eventually reached the ears of Congress.

In 1971, the US Senate Select Committee on Equal Education Opportunity held a series of hearings about the displacement and status of Black school principals in desegregated schools. According to Leon Panetta, director of the US Department of Health, Education, and Welfare (HEW) Office of Civil Rights (OCR) in 1969 during the Nixon administration, concern about the displacement of Black principals had likely come to the Senate as a result of the "NAACP's and other civil and human rights organizations' presence, reach and advocacy" at the time in Washington, DC: "There was strong civil rights leadership in Washington, DC so it makes sense that the issue made it to the Senate."[4] Within a year of being appointed HEW's OCR director, Panetta (who supported school desegregation) was forced out of the Nixon administration after he moved forward with mandated school desegregation efforts more quickly than the administration desired. Panetta was not unlike other officials and citizens who supported the nation's progress on desegregation and rebuked the Nixon administration's irresponsible pandering to "white Southerners *least* reconciled to the ending of an era."

Two of the senators who served on the Select Committee were most likely to have been tapped to bring the issue to hearing: Senator Edward W. Brooke (R-MA) and Senator Walter F. Mondale (D-MN). Brooke (the first Black to be elected to the Senate since the Reconstruction era and from Massachusetts) was concerned about how dual-system states were using the *Brown* decision to illegally fire, demote, and otherwise displace Black

In the aftermath of *Brown* and up until the passage of the Civil Rights Act of 1964, White segregationists were left to their own devices and suppressed any movement to desegregate schools. There were school districts scattered through southern and border states—small and large—that immediately and positively responded to the decree, but their stories are far too often unspoken for at least two reasons: (1) they were the exception rather than the rule, and (2) in some cases, their progress was turned back by protesting White officials and citizens.

Why was there such protracted and violent reaction to desegregation in the dual-system states? In a word, slavery. The Old South depended on its racial caste system, with Blacks trapped at the unabated bottom through the violently coercive enslavement system. The Old South had slavery and all its evil and dehumanizing statutes, customs, and traditions to maintain, police, and sanction White supremacy in every facet of life.

Blacks' enslavement and free labor had transformed colonial economies into a single economy with world preeminence. National and regional leaders knew that the country's burgeoning financial power was linked to the "cotton South—home to the wealthiest counties in the country" prior to the Civil War. Also, from the "cotton South's" soil came political power. Until the Civil War, politicians from southern states had held the presidency for all but thirteen years and had consistently held a majority in Congress and on the Supreme Court.[7] After the Civil War and with ratification of the Thirteenth Amendment (which ended slavery), the South lost its primary engine of wealth and power—more than 6 million enslaved Blacks were freed and poised for full citizenship and rights. The Civil Rights Act of 1866 (the Fourteenth Amendment) guaranteed citizenship regardless of race and previous status as an enslaved person. With this amendment, Blacks could enjoy the legal rights of full citizenship on equal footing as Whites. The Reconstruction Acts of 1867 (the Fifteenth Amendment) granted Black men the right to vote in designated Reconstruction states.[8] This trio of amendments essentially meant that the Old South was largely dead. Although the law facilitated a slow death for the Old South, ideologically nothing had changed. White southern leaders' commitment to Black subjugation remained. The new South that emerged needed segregation and other Jim Crow strictures in order to hang on to vestiges of slavery, a practice that had brutalized and degraded Blacks for centuries by reifying absurd and dangerous beliefs that Blacks despoil Whiteness and White culture and added nothing to civilization and society.

White anger about Black enfranchisement created the new South and fueled adherence to Jim Crow laws enforced by barbaric lynching, intimidation, and economic terrorism. The new South would be defined by segregation in all aspects of Black-White social interactions and access to institutions including schools, transportation, and employment and the ability to purchase land and conduct other financial transactions (on an even playing field). This new order was at once the product of and condition for a new politic—a conservatism that "resisted . . . attempts to redefine the relationship of the federal government to the states and the citizens thereof."[9]

Perhaps more than breaking the segregationist hold on public schools, *Brown* was really aimed at destabilizing White supremacy. Without rigorous enforcement, *Brown* made little progress until the passage of the 1964 Civil Rights Act. The 1964 Act was definitive and clear: discrimination based on race and color was outlawed, as was employment discrimination and racial segregation in schools and public accommodations. With this law came greater Congressional enforcement power. Additionally, the 1964 Civil Rights Act meant that "school districts now had to give due consideration to the fate of [Black educators] after desegregation."[10]

The intervening power of the federal government arrived too late to stop the purge of Black educators after *Brown*. By 1971, the year that the Senate Select Committee on Equal Educational Opportunity convened to consider the displacement and status of Black principals, the damage was proceeding apace. The preliminary counts showed that between 1954 and 1972, 31,584 Black teachers lost their jobs, along with an additional 2,235 Black principals. More data would come in, but it was against this backdrop of recalcitrant White resistance to *Brown* that the Senate convened.

1971: WASHINGTON WEIGHS IN ON BLACK PRINCIPAL AND TEACHER DISPLACEMENT

At 10:00 a.m. on June 14, 1971, only three members of the Select Committee were present: senators Mondale, Ervin, and Hatfield. The first person to present to the Senate Select Committee was Dr. Owen Kiernan, then executive secretary of the National Association of Secondary School Principals

(NASSP), at the time a 35,000-member organization of principals from each of the fifty states and the District of Columbia. In speaking about the status of Black principals, Dr. Kiernan stated:

> There are substantial grounds for concluding that the desegregation of public schools, accompanied by the parallel process of school consolidation, has brought about and continues to result in a marked decrease in the number of Black school principals in almost every southern state. The problem of the elimination, displacement and demotion of Negro public school principals . . . as a result of ongoing desegregation of schools has reached such serious proportions that it requires the intervention of the federal government using its full force and power to bring it to an end.[11]

Kiernan's testimony was followed by that of J. F. Banks, associate director of secondary education in the Virginia State Department of Education. Banks called the decimation of Black principals and teachers "genocide" and asked, "At this rate of decrease, does American education, the basic thrust of our democratic form of government, intend to exclude Blacks from rendering service in this crucial phase of the educational process? Will all the years of pioneering and dedicated service by the Black administrator . . . go to naught and be deleted from its impact upon educational progress?"[12]

These astonishing calls to action by Kiernan and Banks were justified. Plenty of evidence showed that Black principals were being illegally fired, demoted, and dismissed, and the reason for this trend was clear: Black principals were vanishing from border and southern states because control of desegregation was vested in the same power structure that created and retained segregation in the first place. The *Brown* decision and the Civil Rights Act of 1964 provided the legal clout to require states to dismantle the dual system of education and establish a unitary (integrated) system. However, as desegregation progressed in scope and momentum, "it was soon possible to discern a clear and well-defined pattern of discrimination, frightening to behold and devastating in its consequences."[13]

What was being witnessed was active and unabated resistance to *Brown*, the law of the land. Racial discrimination in the hiring, assignment, and promotion of Black principals was proceeding with all deliberate speed. When faced with the requirements of court orders, school districts across the South began programs to decrease the number of Black principals and simultaneously increase the number of White principals. After this purging, few Black principals remained. Whites were already the principals at White schools. With desegregation, they were also appointed as heads of integrated schools and as leaders of the diminishing number of predominantly Black schools. Most Black principals were demoted, fired, or dismissed, while the ranks of White principals swelled exponentially. A minuscule number of Black principals remained. They were uniformly appointed to predominantly Black schools—almost never to predominantly White or integrated schools.

On January 14, 1971, the US Secretary of Health, Education and Welfare (HEW), Elliot L. Richardson, noted it would be "tragic and ironic" if Black educators became the "major victims of the integration effort."[14] And yet this outcome was not unanticipated. Well in advance of Richardson, the National Association for the Advancement of Colored People (NAACP) had begun raising funds to create a Department of Teacher Information and Security in 1952 because it feared that Black principals and teachers would illegally lose their jobs in the battle to integrate schools. According to prominent civil rights leader and NAACP Executive Director Roy Wilkins, safeguarding the jobs, tenure rights, and morale of Black teachers "in the assignment of personnel in desegregated systems" was one of five NAACP priorities.[15] The other four included using the *Brown* decree and the courts to: (1) persuade states and school districts to desegregate in compliance with the *Brown* decision; (2) resist school segregation wherever it was found, including those states and school districts outside of South; (3) "oppose the allocation of any and all forms of federal aid to education to those states or school districts which refuse to comply with the Supreme Court decision"; and (4) "make services available to any Negro parents in any school district who wish to challenge in court those local school authorities who chose to ignore, evade, or openly defy" the *Brown* directives.[16]

John Egerton of the *Southern Education Report* summarized it best as "an unwritten rule that is taking effect all across the southern and border states: When desegregation comes, Negro principals go."[17]

In 1971, data obtained from six border states and eleven southern states confirmed the unwritten rule, as well as Secretary Richardson's and the NAACP's fear. A uniform pattern in seventeen states indicated a methodical pact: *Brown* would be used to abandon whatever vestigial commitment the state had to its Black citizens under the dual system. Schools serving Black students were closed, and legions of Black educators were illegally fired, dismissed, or demoted. Funds that supported Black principals' salaries in the dual system were recaptured and used to hire White principals, whose numbers exponentially increased as the desegregation of the student body progressed. In sum, the approach in county after county, district after district, was to eliminate Black leadership of schools and classrooms in the dual system and phase in White control of the unitary system. For Black principals, this strategy usually meant a dramatic change in status and authority. As J. F. Banks testified, "Sometimes [the Black principal] was reassigned, 'demoted,' to an elementary or junior high school principalship. More often he was removed entirely from policymaking positions."[18]

In the new, unitary system controlled by Whites, Black principals were not to be heads of schools with White teachers and White children, nor were they to lead schools with Black teachers and Black children. The number of White principals was to be increased. Whites were to lead schools serving predominantly White and integrated student bodies. They were also to replace Black principals in the diminishing number of predominantly Black schools. As testimony at the hearings confirmed, "Resistance to the prospect of Black principals supervising White teachers or of Black teachers for White students remains firmly entrenched in southern White communities. As a result, Black educators are being dismissed, removed, or phased out. The Black principal, one dismissed principal commented, is rapidly becoming extinct."[19] The NASSP's Kiernan concurred with this finding; in his testimony before the Senate Select Committee, he concluded that "the very purpose of school desegregation and integration is made a mockery by this treatment of Negro educators."[20]

A sampling of data from different states illustrates the point. For example, Delaware was desegregated in 1967—and that year, the number of Black principals in the state dropped from 50 to 12. Oklahoma had 155 Black principals in 1954, but by 1967 this number had been reduced to 37. In West Virginia, a 1968 sampling estimated that there were 71 Black educators at all levels, almost 200 fewer people than the 1954 total. In Kentucky, the process of desegregation began almost immediately following the 1954 decision, at a time when there about 350 Black principals employed in the state. By 1969, only 36 Black principals remained. In 1954, Maryland had 237 Black principals, a number reduced to 169 by 1968. In 1963, North Carolina had 227 Black principals, but by 1970, there were only 8. During a similar time period, Tennessee reported a reduction from 73 to 17 Black principals statewide. In 1955–1956, Texas was estimated to have 735 Black principals; by 1965–1966, they were down to 558. Virginia reduced its Black principal workforce from 170 to 16 people between 1965 and 1970.[21]

In response to such numbers, the US Department of Education (DOE) concluded that displacement was "delimitating the ranks of Black teachers and threatening Black principals with extinction." DOE associate commissioner Don Davies summarized his agency's findings before the Senate committee in this way: "Our studies suggest a three-fold problem: the demotion of Black principals, a lower rate of hiring of Black teachers, and unemployment among experienced Black teachers and administrators.[22]

MAKING BLACK PRINCIPAL LEADERSHIP EXTINCT

In a riveting account shared with the Senate Select Committee, a Georgia educator, Dr. Bettie M. Smith, explained why the displacement of Black principals constituted a painful and unfair loss of talent to the nation's schools. Like many of her Black peers, Smith was well educated, with a bachelor's degree from historically Black Tennessee Agricultural and Industrial University (now Tennessee State University) and master's and doctoral degrees from New York University. As secretary of the Georgia Council of Secondary School Principals (a Black education association), Smith told the committee that she had seen the organization's membership dwindle from 190 in 1969 to 6 in 1970 because so many Black principals had been removed from their secondary positions "due to the integration situation." Smith went on to explain the relevance of her personal experience to the plight of all Black principals. "I do not speak this morning from a personal standpoint," she testified. "I speak for all the Black principals in the state of Georgia. But I think I can best depict their plight by citing the two experiences I have had as a secondary school principal."[23]

In an exchange with Senator Walter Mondale, a member of the Senate Select Committee, Smith told her compelling story:

SENATOR MONDALE: Do I understand your testimony that—first of all, you hold a doctorate?

DR. SMITH: That is right, Senator, an earned doctorate degree. There have been one or two in the state of Georgia.

SENATOR MONDALE: And you earlier had been a secondary school principal in a school system before you moved to West Point [a junior high school in West Point, Georgia]?

DR. SMITH: Right.

SENATOR MONDALE: And what was the name of that community?

DR. SMITH: Calhoun, Georgia, the Stephens High School, Calhoun, Georgia.

SENATOR MONDALE: You were then demoted to assistant secondary school principal, which you refused to accept?

DR. SMITH: Right.

SENATOR MONDALE: What were the credentials of the principal under whom you were expected to serve?

DR. SMITH: He had a master's degree from the University of Georgia with three years of experience.

SENATOR MONDALE: How many years of experience had you had at that point?

DR. SMITH: At that particular point I had fifteen years in administration.

SENATOR MONDALE: And then you transferred to West Point where you were a secondary school principal?

DR. SMITH: That is right.

SENATOR MONDALE: Until desegregation was ordered and implemented. At that point they transferred you from that position—had they notified you of that or were you on—

DR. SMITH: No, we were not notified. It was merely the order, when they set up the school system that grades nine, ten, eleven, and twelve would be transferred to the former White high school and I would be left with the junior high grades of eight and nine.

SENATOR MONDALE: You were school principal of grades one through eight, then?

DR. SMITH: That is right, until *Calhoun* set in [reference to *Calhoun v. Cook*, 1975]. But when I went to West Point I had strictly secondary grades, eight through twelve.

SENATOR MONDALE: Since that time, you have been ordered from that—first of all, they tried to get you to retire, is that correct?

DR. SMITH: That is right.

SENATOR MONDALE: You refused to do that. Then they made you director of federal programs?

DR. SMITH: That is right.

SENATOR MONDALE: It is your understanding at this point that there is pressure being put on the school board to remove you even from that position, as you testified?

DR. SMITH: That is correct.

SENATOR MONDALE: You must know several other Black secondary school principals in Georgia, do you not, Dr. Smith?

DR. SMITH: I do.

SENATOR MONDALE: Has your experience been unusual or somewhat typical of the kind of treatment?

DR. SMITH: This is typical, Senator, of the pattern of the Black principal, the secondary principal in Georgia; in many instances where he cannot be discredited or disqualified, some little trumped-up charges would be brought up against the majority of them.[24]

Dr. Smith went on to describe the harassment and charges brought against her. She was removed from the principalship while away on an approved study tour in Europe sponsored by the National Association of Secondary School Principals (NASSP). A replacement was appointed to her post. Upon her return, Dr. Smith was pressured by the district superintendent to retire, even though she had been a successful principal and did not have the requisite years for retirement at full pay. When she refused to do so, the superintendent refused to retain her as a principal, and the board of education placed her as a coordinator of federal projects. Once she was placed as federal projects coordinator, dangerous allegations were leveled against her. An anonymous letter to the chair of the board of education stated that she was a Communist. The board chair also received a letter from the board of aldermen and mayor of the city of West Point asking that Smith be denied any job in the West Point public school system because she had led children to revolt and stage demonstrations against the district administration. These accusations were unfounded.

Smith's case and others underscored the conclusion of a state-by-state analysis commissioned by HEW: the Black principal was "desegregation's primary prey."[25] Furthermore, this targeting was purposeful. More often than not, the Black principal was more credentialed and qualified than his or her White counterpart. Furthermore, Black principals played a leading role in the recruitment of Black teachers who comprised the prospective pipeline to school leadership; namely, the principalship. As the dual systems were ordered to close and the ranks of Black principals were reduced, job security for Black teachers in those systems vanished too. When faced with the requirements of court orders to desegregate, school districts decreased the number of Black faculty and simultaneously increased the number of White faculty. The HEW report concluded, "There is enough smoke arising . . . to suspect a big fire—a fire that is decimating the ranks of Black classroom teachers and threatening Black principals with extinction."[26] Even teachers in the principal pipeline were at risk. According to a May 1969 report from the Georgia Teachers and Education Association, Black teachers assigned to Black schools in Gwinnett County, Georgia, were not issued contracts. The teachers protested, and subsequently all but two received contracts. The two who did not "were thought to be potential leaders [and] were just denied their contracts."[27]

The chipping away at the pipeline of prospective Black principals was persistent and pervasive. The fate of Black teachers followed suit. As the NEA noted in an *amicus curiae* brief filed in the Senate hearings, "Even where Black teachers are retained at the high school level, they are often reassigned to lower track and vocationally oriented classes. And almost always, they lose positions as department heads." The NEA brief concluded that data showed that the burden borne during desegregation by Black educators, especially Black principals, was "greatly disproportionate to any burdens borne by White educators."[28]

FIRING BLACK TEACHERS, HIRING WHITE TEACHERS

The 1971 Senate testimony revealed Black teacher firing and White teacher hiring trends in six southern states that painted a familiar—and bleak—picture. Black educators were reduced in proportion to the rates and extent of desegregation, while White educators gained teaching positions at exponential rates. For the two-year period from 1968 to 1970, the number of Black teachers diminished in every state but Florida, while White teachers were hired at increased levels in every state but Mississippi. According to data compiled by the NEA Research Division and HEW and cited in the NEA's

1971 *amicus curiae* brief, the patterns of Black educator displacement were widespread across the southern states:

- Between fall 1968 and fall 1970, Alabama reduced its Black teacher force of 5,264 by 204 people. During the same period, the state reported 10,016 White teachers and increased their ranks by 521.
- In Arkansas, 212 Black teachers lost their jobs in the decade between 1954 and 1968. Between 1954 and 1964, only seven Black teachers were displaced; between 1965 and 1968, 204 lost their jobs. Black male teachers were displaced at a higher rate than Black female teachers between 1954 and 1968.
- Between 1968 and 1970, Florida had 9,463 Black teachers and increased their ranks by 768, while also increasing the ranks of the 39,277 White teachers by 2,965.
- Georgia had 7,687 Black teachers in 1968 and decreased that number by 526. During that same time period, the state had 22,943 White teachers and increased their ranks by 1,086.
- Louisiana reduced the number of Black teachers by 519 from 11,781 while increasing the number of White teachers by nineteen from 21,827.
- Mississippi decreased the number of Black teachers by 599 from 7,162 and decreased the number of White teachers by 399 from 9,543.
- Texas had 12,307 Black teachers in 1969 and reduced their ranks by 32. The state had 67,567 White teachers and increased their ranks by 1,383.[29]

In his 1970 dissertation, *Status and Characteristics of Displaced Negro Teachers in Arkansas, 1954–1968*, Dr. Albert Baxter warned that, given the shakeup in the profession, a large number of potential Black teachers would be discouraged from entering the field and the states would "lose a resource which is eminently qualified to resolve the problems incident to desegregation."[30] A 1969 report from the Georgia Teachers and Education Association (GTEA) reached similar conclusions, stating that the "continued loss of professional positions will discourage Black students from aspiring to become teachers and other professionals." The GTEA charged that the practice of firing must be halted and reversed because "this nation and the state need all good teachers," and Georgia could not afford to lose 25 percent of its trained and experienced educators.[31]

These state-by-state atrocities led then-HEW Secretary Elliot Richardson to conclude in his Senate testimony that "the treatment of [Black] teachers is one of the major problems remaining after the merger of the dual school system."[32]

The NEA's *amicus curiae* brief pointed out that the decimation of the Black educator pipeline was not fully depicted by a mere "body count" of those displaced. Rather, other surveys indicated that the elimination of Black principals and teachers was even more pronounced than the data from HEW disclosed. Such displacement could only fully be measured, the NEA observed, by the "detrimental effect upon Black children" who "had a right to desegregated schooling including desegregated faculties."[33] NEA doubled down on its defense of Black principals and teachers, affirming that the organization "will continue to oppose vigorously desegregation plans and practices that result in the systematic displacement or demotion of Black principals and teachers. It urges federal agencies charged with approving and enforcing plans to do the same."[34]

A variety of methods were used to relieve Black teachers of their posts. First and foremost was the closing of Black schools. Along with school closures came outright illegal firing, denial and nonrenewal of contracts, and pressure for early retirement or resignation. During this time, NAACP Legal Defense and Educational Fund (LDF) monitors reported that many Black teachers received letters from superintendents and principals indicating that "because of a desegregation mandate, their jobs could not be guaranteed."[35] Black educators who resisted illegal demotions and firing were subjected to an extraordinary range of reprisals: physical threats and other violence, cancellation of store credit, removal of department head titles, demotion from high school to junior high or elementary schools, out-of-subject placement, elimination through National Teacher Examination (NTE) testing, and "promotion" (i.e., sidelining) to district-based federally funded programs.

In the latter case, Black teachers were "promoted" to head federally funded programs such as those under Title I of the Elementary and Secondary Act of 1964. In some districts, Black teachers were the only professionals appointed to federal program posts, thereby making them easier targets for dismissal. When federal money ran low or was revoked from districts for noncompliance with federal mandates, "promoted" Black teachers were released. Some states anticipating lawsuits even repealed their continuing contract laws. In states with no statewide tenure laws, Black teachers were particularly vulnerable because "contracts are generally let on a yearly basis and so White principals have an annual opportunity to recommend the elimination of any Black teacher from the faculty," observed the NEA.[36]

During the years following the *Brown* decision, with Black principals virtually nowhere on the scene, White principals were free to manipulate Black teachers' hiring, school placements, and course assignments. As head of the LDF in 1955, Thurgood Marshall noticed that tenure laws protected approximately 43 percent of southern schoolteachers and that it was rumored these statutes would be repealed if schools were integrated.[37] Marshall documented his findings in a memorandum titled "A Program to Protect Negro Teachers from Dismissal as a Result of the Integration of Public Schools." Among other examples, he observed that in rural Georgia, "an extreme instance of intimidation" occurred shortly after the *Brown* decision, with Black teachers being "used as a weapon to delay desegregation." He wrote: "When time for annual renewal of teachers' contracts arrived, each Negro teacher was handed an unsigned contract and a petition form addressed to local officials. It was understood that only after the teacher had secured signatures of parents to the petition, requesting that their children remain in all-Negro schools, would the teacher's contract be renewed for the coming year."[38]

In Franklin County, South Carolina, Black teachers received a letter from the superintendent stating that they were being terminated immediately because their principal did not recommend them for appointment. All were serving under White principals who typically had been appointed after the school's Black principal was demoted or fired.[39] Dr. Benjamin Epstein, a New Jersey assistant superintendent, spoke eloquently at the hearings in his role as chairman of the status and welfare committee of the NASSP. "What happened to the Black educator involved?" he asked. "Many were forced into early, premature retirements. Others were demoted. Still others were just plain fired. A few were given respite in the form of jobs in school system central offices so long as they were not actively in charge of integrated schools."[40]

Black teachers who were illegally fired and court-ordered to be rehired were routinely consigned to hall duty and study halls rather than their old classrooms. Titles never before used in schools, such as "assistant visiting teacher," became the vogue for demoted but rehired Black teachers. Another strategy documented by an NEA task force was to segregate teacher and student assignments within the merged, nominally "integrated" schools. In fact, Black teachers and students were "departmentalized even at the elementary level (presumably so that a White child would not be with a Black teacher all day)."[41] In other cases, Black teachers were required to teach subjects out of their discipline and then fired for incompetence. In 1970, HEW found that Blacks were made co-teachers with "domineering Whites," "teacher's aides with no responsibility," and "floating teachers without a classroom of their own." Marvin Davies, a field director for the NAACP in Florida, observed: "Many Black teachers now 'just babysit.' They stand watch in halls or in the cafeteria, and they watch the kids get on and off the buses."[42]

Black teachers fielded other assaults on their professional competence, too. White superintendents and principals alleged that Blacks were unqualified, even though by 1949–1950, Black teacher training exceeded that of Whites in Washington, DC, and seven of twelve border and southern states, including Maryland, Oklahoma, Texas, Virginia, South Carolina, Florida, and West Virginia. In his study of the teaching force, the noted African American scholar W. E. B. Du Bois, generally viewed as the father of American sociology, described White teachers as "not as good as the Negro teachers." Other researchers argued that the credentials of Black teachers had been obscured because Black teachers "found it necessary to understate their qualifications to be hired by White school boards."[43]

Over time, the harassment and humiliation that accompanied African American educator demotions had a quantifiable impact on their numbers. As the 1970 HEW-commissioned report on Black teacher displacement put it, "Some of these [Black] teachers give up and resign. Some protest and are fired for insubordination. And into the places of these demoted and dismissed Blacks, more often than not, go Whites—some with less education and experience than the teachers they are replacing."[44]

Cautioning that "the elimination of Black teachers must be reversed," the GTEA concluded that "this nation and state need all good teachers" and "cannot afford to lose more than a quarter of its teachers."[45]

Yet despite extensive cautionary notes, documentation, and copious reports, illegal treatment of Black teachers continued. Mistreatment was so widespread that two NEA fact-finding teams recommended that the association undertake legal assistance to prevent and defend against desegregation-related infringements on the rights of Black educators. In 1970, the NEA published *Desegregation and the Rights of Educators in Louisiana*, a guide offering legal advice to displaced Black principals and teachers. It provides a glimpse into problems frequently encountered by Black educators during the era. Though southern states then and now are "right-to-work states" with weak unions and worker rights, the NEA guide is a testament to how Black educators' fight for fairness expanded all educators' rights and strengthened their collective bargaining power.

The publication answered 52 frequently asked questions in each of four areas. Taken together, the topics and questions reveal the extraordinary levels of opposition Black educators faced in retaining their jobs and protecting their careers during this tumultuous time:

- **Personal Rights and Freedoms:** Does an educator have the right to engage in political activity? Is an educator protected against dismissal or other sanction if he reports violations of the law with respect to the operation of the school—such as misallocation of Title I funds or violations of desegregation orders? What remedies does an educator have if he is subjected to criminal arrest for exercising voting rights, rights of free speech, the right to publicly protest, assemble or demonstrate, or other constitutionally protected rights? Does an educator exercising or contemplating the exercise of such rights have a remedy against threats or reprisals by private individuals taking such forms as eviction, withdrawal of credit, or foreclosure or repossession of property?
- **Rights of Teachers Against Unreasonable Official Directives and Other Intrusions:** May a teacher's person or belongings be searched on or off the premises of the school by school authorities or law enforcement officials? Can a school administrator legally use wiretaps or other electronic devices to monitor his conference with a teacher? Does a teacher have a right to refuse or to eject from his classroom a student who is harassing the teacher or other students with racial slurs or epithets or for racial reasons?
- **Legal Protections Against Displacement as a Result of Desegregation (the Singleton Decree):** In the event of a reduction in force, what protection does a teacher have against arbitrary dismissal or demotion by the school authorities? What protections does an educator have against racially discriminatory dismissal or demotion as a result of a

reduction in force incident to school desegregation? What can teachers and principals do to ensure that the selection of professional staff for dismissal or demotion incident to school desegregation is in fact made on the basis of objective and reasonable nondiscriminatory criteria? Can a school system require in-service teachers or applicants for teaching positions to achieve a minimum score on the National Teachers' Examination or other tests as a condition of retention or employment? Many Black educators are dismissed or demoted after their schools have been phased out or closed. Can Black educators do anything to secure the continuing use of adequate existing facilities?

- **Protections Against Unjust Dismissals, Demotions, and Reassignments:** What protections do educators have against racially discriminatory dismissals, demotions, and other types of discrimination by their school boards? Can an educator be dismissed because he has been convicted of a traffic violation? What protection does an educator in Louisiana have against a demotion taking the form of a contract renewal at lesser pay, status, or responsibility? When does a board of education have a legal right to demote an educator? Does an educator have the right to retain his own lawyer when threatened with dismissal, demotion, or other adverse action by a school system? Does an educator have a legal right to know the number of days to be worked and the amount of compensation to be received when entering into a contract? Are teachers whose contracts identify them as "Title I" or "Project" or "ESEA" teachers protected against dismissal or demotion when federal funds are exhausted? Can a teacher refuse reassignment to the status of a "Title I" "Project" or "ESEA" teacher? What relief can a teacher obtain from a court if he is discharged or substantially disadvantaged contrary to his rights?[46]

ANOTHER BLOW: UNFAIR HIRING PRACTICES

In many ways, the unfair hiring practices experienced by Black teachers posed an even bigger threat to their ranks than firings. As the HEW report noted, "The large reservoir of unemployed [Black] teachers is as symptomatic of the decline in hiring as it is of displacement."[47] Several other studies concurred with this conclusion. In its survey of 108 southern school districts, the Atlanta Office for Civil Rights found that 3,774 White teachers

(77 percent) and 1,133 Black teachers (23 percent) left their school systems during the fall of 1968. Only 14 percent of new hires (743 educators) were Black. The remaining 86 percent (4,453 people) were White. NEA's *amicus curiae* brief filed on behalf of Black teachers in Georgia noted that even those school districts in the then–Fifth Circuit (Alabama, Florida, Georgia, Louisiana, Mississippi, and Texas) under court order had "virtually stopped hiring Black educators":

> In Starkville, Mississippi, the school district hired 32 White teachers and no Black teachers for 1970 though Black teachers comprised 29.8 percent of the faculty the preceding year. . . . In Columbus, Mississippi, the school district hired 29 White teachers and one Black teacher for 1970 although Black teachers comprised 35.4 percent of the faculty in the preceding year. . . . Concordia [Louisiana] Parish hired 26 new White teachers and no Black teachers for 1970, although Black teachers comprised 48.5 percent of the Parish's faculty. Limestone County, Alabama, in the past two years hired two Black teachers out of 65. In 1968 the Black teachers comprised 22 percent of the County's teaching force. Chilton County in 1968–69 hired 33 new White teachers and 13 new Black teachers. In 1969–70, the Board hired 27 new White teachers and two new Black teachers. For the 1970–71 school year, the board has hired 19 new White teachers and no Black teachers.[48]

In a report about the lack of hiring of newly prepared Black teachers in Texas, the Commission on Democracy in Education found that "new Black teachers do not enjoy equal opportunity at available teaching positions. In the small school districts, there is a notable decrease in employment of Black teachers; some have not employed any Black teachers during the past two years."[49]

Texas was not the only state discouraging young Blacks from teaching. E. Harper Johnson, director of special services and staff consultant for human relations with the Tennessee Education Association, described "a trend against employing young Blacks." Hayes Mizell of the South Carolina Education Association cautioned, "It is a problem to be on the lookout for—after desegregation, Blacks just aren't getting hired." Alluding to the problem getting worse and not better, John Gadsden, executive director of Penn Community Services in South Carolina, observed, "School systems are only doing a minimum of what they have to do. There is a fear on the part of [Black] teachers over the next stage, when school systems get bolder" in eliminating them.[50]

Much of the data on Black educator displacement came to light through research conducted by the Nashville-based Race Relations Information Center (RRIC), founded as the Southern Education Reporting Service and funded in 1954 by the Ford Foundation to collect unbiased data and information about Southern school desegregation. An interracial organization, the RRIC operated under a board of directors including presidents of three HBCUs—Tuskegee University, Fisk University, and Talladega College—as well as the famed Howard University sociologist Dr. Andrew Billingsley, who at the time served as Howard's Vice President for Academic Affairs. Other board members included the chancellor of Vanderbilt University and George Peabody College; faculty members from Harvard, Columbia, and Pennsylvania State Universities; Lerone Bennett, the editor of *Ebony Magazine;* the editors of two Black newspapers, the *Chicago Defender* and the *St. Louis Sentinel*; Wallace Westfeldt, executive producer of NBC *Nightly News*; and Vernon Jordan, executive director of the United Negro College Fund.

RRIC's report, *The Displacement of Black Teachers in the Eleven Southern States* (1970), was authored by staff member Robert Hooker. Hooker summarized the state-by-state trends in Black educator firing and hiring across the South and shared accounts by local officials about their circumstances. With examples of six Black teachers (of fifty-four total) hired in Rocky Mount and three Black teachers (of forty total) hired in Washington, North Carolina, E. B. Palmer, associate executive director of the North Carolina Teachers Association, concluded that the pattern of hiring White teachers rather than Black ones was "true all over the state." In summarizing the hiring forecast for White teachers, Hooker observed that "all sources concede that White prospects are probably better." James Burch, a North Carolina state department of education official, summarized the situation aptly when he said, "If you put a White and a Black side by side, the White will be the one hired."[51]

Similarly, LDF investigator Bob Valder reported, "I have seen virtually no district where there was hiring to keep the teacher ratio comparable to the student ratio or even the current teacher ratio. I would lay odds that it's happening in the rest of the South, too."[52]

A Florida Education Association (FEA) report reached a startling conclusion: The more Black students were integrated, the fewer Black teachers were hired. Wally Johnson, FEA's executive secretary, described the operating ratio in this way: Over a three-year period, the total number of teachers in the state rose by 7,500. For every twenty-two new Black pupils to enter Florida schools during that period, one Black educator disappeared.[53]

State by state, attorneys litigating on behalf of Black teachers told the RRIC researchers that employment prospects for Black teachers were very poor, especially when compared with those of their White peers. Solomon Seay, a Montgomery attorney, concluded: "The trend for 1970–1971 is that lots of systems just aren't hiring new Blacks." In Monroe, Louisiana, attorney Paul Kidd predicted, "Inside of four years, I doubt there'll be 10 percent of our Black teaches still left in the state." John Walker, a Little Rock, Arkansas, attorney, flatly asserted: "Almost every district has something" resulting in the loss of Black educators. Ruth Harvey, a Danville, Virginia, attorney and member of the State Advisory Committee to the US Civil Rights Commission, reported Black educator displacements throughout the state. "Yes, most definitely, it's happening" agreed Henry L. Marsh III, Richmond attorney and vice mayor. Atlanta Attorney Howard Moore told the RRIC investigators, "I believe they were fired because districts are cutting back on Black teachers and principals." Theodore Bowers, an attorney in Panama City, noted widespread discrimination, including outright dismissals and substantial demotions in a seven-county area of Florida.[54]

Attorney Conrad Harper of the LDF, which litigated the highest number of cases on behalf of Black educators, explained, "The problem has become epidemic. Increasingly the trend is popping up all over the place."[55] Dr. Albert Baxter summarized it best in his comment about the lies conceived to fire qualified Black educators: "If I had a degree from the Sorbonne," Dr. Baxter wrote, "my education would be 'inferior' because I am Black."[56]

Yet in response to interrogation about the dearth of Black teacher hires, White superintendents claimed that Blacks were just not applying for teaching posts. A report from the Commission on Democracy in Education partially confirmed this assertion—though not because Black educators were finding other opportunities. Rather, the commission report concluded, "their employment prospects are so poor they don't bother to apply," and they were "discouraged by the prospect of being shifted from school to school."[57]

Such was the case for longtime educator Virgil Coleman of Elba, Alabama. Coleman had been principal of the all-Black Warren Smith High School for eighteen years when, after the desegregation mandate, he was reassigned to the principalship of an elementary school. After serving for two weeks, he was removed and appointed assistant principal of a newly merged high school, New Brockton High School. In this position, his primary responsibility was defined as "disciplining Black students."[58] In North Carolina, one county superintendent required Black teachers to teach in a summer enrichment program at half salary so that he could observe them and ascertain their level of competence to teach in the unitary school system. White teachers were subjected to no such scrutiny of their fitness for the unitary system or their competence to teach Black students.

RURAL VERSUS URBAN SCHOOLS

Schooling in the United States has always been a mainly rural phenomenon. Nearly 70 percent of school districts (9,642 of 13,800) are in rural settings or small towns. Fewer than 4,000 of the nation's school districts are in suburban settings, and fewer than 1,000 are categorized as urban.[59]

As the desegregation of schools progressed in the last decades of the twentieth century, Black teachers fared a bit better in large city districts than in the small town and county school systems that populated the rural South and composed the majority of the nation's school systems. Like the decline in the hiring of Black educators, the demotions and firings of Blacks were more a rural phenomenon than an urban one and were most widespread in the deep southern states of Mississippi, Louisiana, and Alabama. In these settings, charged Dr. Albert G. Tippitt (a Black principal whose University of Virginia dissertation was about Black principal displacement), "there won't be any Black replacements unless the Black is Phi Beta Kappa. And how many Phi Beta Kappas would want to locate in, say, Crossbone County?"[60] In rural Mississippi, Rims Barber, the executive director of the Delta Ministry of the National Council of Churches, one of Mississippi's largest interracial civil rights groups, reported that 80 percent of the new teachers hired in twenty-six Mississippi districts were White. "A year or two ago," said Barber, "that percentage was 50 or 60 percent."[61] Mississippi's Black teachers and community were not alone in their concern about the growing displacement of Black teachers by Whites in the unitary system. In an exceptional show of solidarity and activism, 110 of the 120 Black teachers in Kinston, North Carolina, retained an attorney, Donald Pollock, to investigate teacher hiring trends. In summarizing the teachers' concerns, he stated, "They want to know why, in a school where Black students are more than 50 percent, Black teachers are less than 30 percent." The pattern was noticeable elsewhere too. In King George County, Virginia, twenty-two new White teachers were hired, but only one new Black teacher. In this district, where the student population was nearly 50 percent Black, the faculty was estimated to be less than 15 percent Black. The Georgia Teachers and Education Association offered a warning about the failure to integrate Black educators in its report *How the Elimination of the Dual School System is Affecting Negro Educators in 30 Selected School Systems in North Georgia*: "This trend must not only be halted. It must be reversed. Integration must mean the inclusion of Black professionals at least equal to the proportion of Black students in each system. . . . If this trend is not stopped now, it will continue, probably at an accelerated pace."[62]

It was not uncommon for southern school districts to have majority Black student populations, particularly in rural locales. Despite this demographic reality, when faced with the requirements of court orders, most of these districts began a program to decrease the number of Black faculty and simultaneously increase the number of White faculty. Such was the case with the majority-Black school district in Baker County, Georgia. During the 1969–1970 school year, the district enrolled 1,062 students, 711 (67 percent) of whom were Black and 351 of whom were White. During that year, 92.5 percent of Black students attended two all-Black schools, while all the district's White students attended one school having twelve grades. When the district was mandated to end segregation, the percentage of Black teachers decreased from 59 percent in 1969–1970 to 48 percent in 1970–1971. This reduction in Black teachers occurred under a stated district plan to reduce its Black faculty by eleven and increase its White faculty by ten, even though the districts' White student population dropped by 131 students that year.[63]

In explaining his decision to deviate from the court order and the district's plan (which already called for the reduction of Black teachers and the hiring of more White teachers), Baker County's (White) superintendent testified that he believed that the court order was designed to allow school systems to alter their Black-White faculty ratios through hiring and firing, and that furthermore, he was of the opinion that White teachers were more competent than Blacks. He therefore decided to change the systemwide teacher ratio from nearly 60 percent Black to 60 percent White.

Only one weapon was "more powerful than" the White principal's power to declare the Black teacher incompetent, and that was the National Teacher

Examination (NTE).[64] During desegregation's heyday, about 40 percent of the test's use was in the southeastern states. The NEA and Black educators noticed the increased use of the test in southern states and concluded that it was being used as "a punitive measure to justify the racial imbalance in hiring practices."[65] For the first time, state-derived cutoff scores were linked to teacher certification and, in some cases, salary level. Dr. Richard Majestic, NTE program director for the Educational Testing Service, recognized that the NTE was being used to rid southern systems of Black teachers. "You can build the best test available," he said, "but if there's malice in somebody's heart, it can be used to eliminate Blacks." Interestingly, Florida dropped use of the NTE after the mid-1960s, when larger-than-expected percentages of White teachers failed to reach the cutoff score.[66]

Throughout the South, a "not-fired-but-not-hired refrain" was heard loud and clear for Black educators. The result, according to J. Shelby Guss, a Virginia Education Association official, was that "our [Black] young people just aren't turning toward teaching like they used to."[67] Baxter's 1970 dissertation predicted the same: "If employment tendencies inferred from the findings in this study continue, a large number of potential Negro teachers will be discouraged from entering the teaching profession. Thus, the state of Arkansas will lose a resource which is eminently qualified to help resolve the problems incident to desegregation."[68]

HEW confirmed the bad news. Its multistate study found "considerable unemployment reported among 1965 Negro college graduates prepared to teach." It concluded that the cost of integration to Black educators and communities was too exacting: "The price of desegregation often has been the pay or the prestige or the position of the Black [educator] . . . What J. C. James in the *New Republic* called 'the greatest single reservoir of talent and skills so necessary to the changing South' is clearly in danger of marked depletion, if not eventual extinction. And that, for the desegregating South and its Black community, may be the cruelest irony of all."[69]

Dr. Albert Baxter's final recommendation in his dissertation was prophetic. In his study about the displacement of Black teachers in Arkansas, he urged that "when total desegregation of Arkansas' public schools has occurred, a similar study [should] be undertaken to complete the story of Negro teacher displacement."[70] In 1954–1955, there were 124 Black secondary school principals and by 1970–1971, the ranks had been wiped out to fourteen. There was not one Black principal appointed to Arkansas's (biracial) desegregating schools. At the time of the Supreme Court decision in 1954, there were approximately 1,550 Black principals in Oklahoma. By 1967, this number had been reduced by approximately 75 percent to only 37 people. In 1954, there were 350 Black principals leading Kentucky public schools. By 1969–1970, only 36 remained.

No matter who issued the study, the method of desegregation used by dual-system states had "baneful consequences" for Black principals and teachers and remarkable benefits for White principals.[71] Georgia was typical of the dual-system states when it reported that its Black principal workforce dropped 55 percent in thirty reporting districts from 54 in 1963–1964 to 24 in 1968–1969, while the number of White principals in the same districts grew that year from 284 to 308 (an 8 percent increase).

As public school desegregation gradually made its way across the South in the 1960s and 1970s, Jim Crow was indeed dying—though far too slowly. Remarkably, he steadily issued pink slips to Black principals and teachers and kept devising other devious schemes to take these educators to the grave with him.

2

THE MYTH OF BLACK PROFESSIONAL INFERIORITY

> *Since Black principals tend to be more qualified than White principals with respect to degree and certification status, it is necessary for those who appoint principals to provide data that would explain why the discrepancy between Black and White principal [appointments] exist[s].*
>
> —Maryland State Department of Education, 1969

> *There are substantial grounds for concluding that the desegregation of public schools, accompanied by the parallel process of school consolidation, has brought about and continues to result in a marked decrease in the number of Black school principals in almost every Southern State.*
>
> —Dr. Owen Kiernan
> National Association of Secondary School Principals, 1970

> *Demotion of Black administrators is the rule . . .*
>
> —NEA report, 1970

JIM CROW'S ODD, unprovoked, and evil conspiracies sometimes backfired and unwittingly gave the advantage to Blacks. Prior to and after the *Brown* decision, the "separate but equal" reach of 1896's *Plessey v. Ferguson* could still be felt. Seventeen states had constitutions with racial lines drawn providing that "White and colored children" not be taught in the same schools. In these jurisdictions, statutory provisions prohibited the education of Blacks alongside Whites from elementary school through college, graduate, and professional schools. Blacks were unable to attend taxpayer-funded public colleges and universities that, under the segregated system, were reserved for Whites. Instead, Black residents seeking a college education attended state-supported and private historically Black colleges/universities (HBCUs). However, only a few HBCUs—most notably Howard University, Fisk University, Atlanta University, Meharry Medical College, and Tuskegee Institute—provided graduate and professional education. In seventeen states, Black residents desiring to attend graduate school could only attend HBCUs, so if the course of study desired (for instance, a PhD in educational administration) was unavailable at an in-state HBCU, the prospective Black graduate student had to leave the state of his or her residence to attend an integrated university, usually located in one of the northeastern or midwestern states. The data show that, overwhelmingly, these Black educators forced out of their home states for graduate degrees often enrolled in some of the most highly ranked universities in the nation.

BLACK EDUCATORS LOCKED OUT OF SOUTHERN WHITE-RESERVED PUBLIC COLLEGES AND UNIVERSITIES

The dual-system states that denied college and graduate school admission to Black citizens argued that the out-of-state financial aid provisions for Blacks "did not deprive the Negro of his rights under the Fourteenth Amendment because the state paid nonresident tuition in the form of out-of-state scholarships for Negro students desiring work not offered at one of the state's HBCUs."[1] In fact, the segregationist states were knowingly bucking two judicial decisions: *Murray v. Pearson* (1936) and *State of Missouri ex rel. Gaines v. Canada et al.* (1938). Both of these cases were part of the long march of arguments against "separate but equal" doctrines that provided the foundation for a racially segregated society before the 1954 *Brown* decision declared racial segregation illegal in public schools, colleges, and universities.

The first decision came in *Murray v. Pearson* (1936), mandating that racially restrictive states cease being so and admit qualified Blacks to their graduate school programs. The *Murray* case had been argued by Thurgood Marshall on behalf of Donald G. Murray, a Black graduate of Amherst, who was denied admission to the University of Maryland Law School on the basis of race. The judge hearing the case ruled that Murray had been rejected solely because of his race and ordered the university to admit him. Murray became the first Black graduate of the Maryland law school in 1938.

The second legal decision the segregationist states skirted around was rendered in *State of Missouri ex rel. Gaines v. Canada et al.* (1938), in which the US Supreme Court ruled that forcing citizens out of state to attend graduate programs just because they were Black was a violation of the Fourteenth Amendment's equal protection clause prohibiting discrimination and ensuring equal protection under the law. The 6-2 decision was a pyrrhic victory—a win in principle that concluded that the state must provide Black students access to a state law school but, in broader terms, a loss because the decision did not overturn the segregationist law that prevented Blacks from attending the University of Missouri School Law School. In short, the case upheld the separate-but-equal doctrine by concluding that segregationist states either had to build separate graduate schools for Blacks or integrate. Interestingly, Justice Hugo Black was one of those hearing the case. Justice Black, who later supported the *Brown* decision, held a lifetime membership (which he said he disavowed before being appointed to the court) in the Ku Klux Klan (KKK), a White terrorist organization guilty of murdering and violently harassing thousands of innocent Black men, women, and children; carrying out a hate campaigns against Jewish people; and opposing the civil rights movement and integration in American society.

The Missouri law school case was brought by Lloyd Gaines, a graduate of Missouri's Lincoln University (a state-supported HBCU), who sought admission to the University of Missouri School of Law but was denied admission by the university's registrar, S. W. Canada, because state law prohibited Blacks from attending the school. After refusing the university's offer to provide a "Negro tuition scholarship" to send him to a neighboring state's law school (Iowa or Kansas) with no racial restriction, Gaines filed suit on the recommendation of a former college professor, who referred him to the NAACP.

The case was litigated twice—first at the circuit court and then at the State Supreme Court—before it went to the US Supreme Court in 1938. Each time, the case was tried by an all-White male establishment, including circuit court and state Supreme Court judges who were graduates of the University of Missouri. As the case went through the courts, the state of Missouri hurriedly went about establishing a law school for Blacks at Lincoln University in a blatant attempt to retain its commitment to separate-but-equal. In the meantime, like many Black principals and teachers, Gaines left his home state of Missouri and went north to earn a graduate degree. In 1937, he earned a master's degree in economics from the University of Michigan as he awaited resolution of his case.

In an effort to destroy the "separate but equal" doctrine that the Supreme Court had upheld in its 1938 decision, Charles Hamilton Houston and the NAACP team of attorneys returned to Missouri to build a new case. Again, Lloyd Gaines was to be the key plaintiff—but then, suddenly and mysteriously, he went missing.

Gaines's last letter to his mother was written on March 3, 1939. It provides an intimate glimpse into what was on his mind and heart. He wrote that he was frustrated and regretted that the only work that he could find was as a gas station attendant, even though he held a bachelor's degree with honors from Lincoln University and a master's degree in economics from the University of Michigan. He was weary and worn out from the lawsuits, the publicity and notoriety that he experienced as a result, and the financial drain imposed on his mother and brother as they supported him through it all. Though exhausted by the constrictions of segregated life and the personal demands of the cause for which he was fighting, he described himself as willingly making a "supreme sacrifice" so that, as he said, "thirteen million Negroes" could have a right to an integrated education in their own states of residence.

Gaines went on to express to his mother how happy it made him to receive an enthusiastic reception from a crowd of 1,400 Black supporters (with hundreds being turned away) in Kansas City, Kansas, where he gave a speech. He told his mother that he had "never been met with such hospitality and friendship" and that the crowd kept him an hour after his speech requesting autographs and handshakes. Despite all that he had experienced at the hand of racism and Jim Crow, when he delivered remarks later that Monday at Sumner High School, a noted all-Black high school in Kansas City, he told his mother that in his two addresses he spoke about the "elements of unity and cooperation" and "choosing and achieving your purpose in life." Clearly, there was no malice in the messages Gaines delivered, though given his experiences, he could have shared a message of hurt, anger, and hate. Instead, he focused on uplift.

In the end, Lloyd Gaines never graduated from the University of Missouri School of Law. Instead, he disappeared and was never found. Some say his disappearance was tied to the KKK, which was believed to have killed him. Others speculated that the court cases had taken too much of a psychological and financial toll, leading him to escape it all and take refuge in Mexico. In their research into Gaines's fate, University of Missouri's law school librarians Needra Jackson and Cynthia Basset conclude from library records that it is highly likely that physical harm came to Gaines and that he was unlikely to abruptly sever communication with his mother and brother, with whom he was very close and with whom he had corresponded regularly via letter and Western Union. Mindful of the racially motivated lynchings, murders, and other deaths that marked the era, in 1940 and again in 1970, Gaines's family members requested that the Federal Bureau of Investigation (FBI) investigate his disappearance. Twice the FBI declined.

Whatever Gaines's fate, the racist circumstances surrounding his life exacted much from him and his family. His stellar academic record warranted his acceptance to the University of Missouri School of Law. Had he been a White citizen of the state, he would have been admitted.

NEGRO TUITION SCHOLARSHIPS TO TOP-TIER GRADUATE SCHOOLS

Until the mid-twentieth century, all but six of the seventeen dual-system states provided budget allocations to send qualified Black students out of state for graduate school in selected fields. Despite the *Murray* and *Gaines* decisions in 1935 and 1938, dual-system states continued to circumvent the law and approve state statutes and budgets for tuition subsidies to send Black graduate students out of state. In fact, the 1938 *Gaines* decision appeared to have ushered in a new enthusiasm for this practice in the segregationist states. In 1939, Black scholarship allocations for ten states grew immediately by 88.3 percent from $67,500.00 to $127,123.31. In the ensuing years up to 1943, growth increased by 36.9 percent.[2] In addition to tuition and fees, some states even paid transportation and living allowance stipends. Between 1927 and 1941, state statutes governing these allocations proliferated like a game of tag between neighboring states as recalcitrant governors and state legislators refused to desegregate and sought ways to shift Black graduate education across state lines.

In an article published in the *Journal of Negro Education* in 1944, Reid E. Jackson offered the first detailed analysis of Negro tuition scholarships from this period. Jackson charted his findings in three tables (see tables 2.1 and 2.2) describing the dual-system state statutes' parameters, grant award amounts, and oversight of these monies.[3]

A third table summarized "Basic Requirements for Scope of Grants by Certain Southern States to Negroes for Out-of-State Study." As Jackson documented, the process for the tuition awards was typically overseen by

TABLE 2.1 Provisions by the State Maintaining Segregated Educational Systems for Out-of-State Study by Negroes

STATE	DATE OF LEGISLATION	AREA OF STUDY	ANNUAL APPROPRIATION ($)[1]
1. Alabama	None		
2. Arkansas	1943	All courses not available in Negro state college[2]	5,000
3. Delaware	None		
4. Florida	None		
5. Georgia	None		
6. Kentucky	1936	All courses offered at White state institutions but not available in Negro state college	10,000
7. Louisiana	None		
8. Maryland	1935	All courses offered at White state university but not available in Negro state college	25,000
9. Mississippi	None		
10. Missouri	1929	All courses offered at White state university but not available in Negro state college	30,000
11. North Carolina	1939	All courses offered at White state university but not available in Negro state college	15,000
12. Oklahoma	1941[3]	All courses offered at White state institutions but not available in Negro state colleges	15,000
13. South Carolina	None		
14. Tennessee	1941	All courses offered at White state university but not available in Negro state college	No data
15. Texas	1939	Graduate and professional courses offered in White state institutions but not available at Negro state college	25,000
16. Virginia	1936	Graduate and professional courses offered in White state institutions but not available at Negro state colleges	40,000
17. West Virginia	1927	All courses available at any state institution from which Negroes are debarred	9,000

Source: Reid E. Jackson, "Financial Aid Given by Southern States to Negroes for Out-of-State Study," *Journal of Negro Education* 13, no. 1 (1944): 30–39.

[1] Figures in this column represent the last annual appropriation.
[2] This would include undergraduate as well as graduate and professional courses.
[3] Appropriations were begun in Oklahoma in 1937, before enactment of legislative approval.

TABLE 2.2 The Administration of Out-of-State Scholarship Programs for Negroes in Certain Southern States, as to Type and Disbursement

STATE	TYPE OF ADMINISTRATIVE CONTROL	KINDS OF CREDENTIAL FORMS	MODE OF DISBURSEMENT
1. Arkansas	State board of education	1. Forms not yet available	By voucher from state board of education
2. Kentucky	State board of education through president of Negro state college	1. Application blank 2. Official transcript 3. Affidavit of citizenship	By state voucher to the institution
3. Maryland	Board of Trustees for Negro state college	1. Application blank 2. Official transcript 3. Recommendation letters 4. Health certificate 5. Photograph 6. Personal interview	By check from scholarship commission secretary to student
4. Missouri	Board of Curators for Negro state college	1. Application blank 2. Official admit card 3. Recommendation letters	State warrant payable for student forwarded to institution for delivery to student upon completing registration
5. North Carolina	Board of Trustees for Negro state college	1. Application blank 2. Official admit card	1. Check for fees from administering agent to institution 2. Check for travel directly to student
6. Oklahoma	State board of education	1. Application blank 2. Official transcript 3. Personal history	By voucher from state board of education to student
7. Tennessee	State board of education through coordinator of higher education for Negroes	1. Application blank 2. Official transcript 3. Affidavit of citizenship 4. Recommendation letters	By voucher from state board of education to the institution
8. Texas	Committee of graduate deans from White state colleges	1. Application blank 2. Official transcript 3. Recommendation letters 4. Official admit card	State warrant payable to student forwarded to institution for delivery to student upon completing registration
9. Virginia	State board of education	1. Application blank 2. Official transcript 3. Recommendation letters 4. Health certificates	By treasurer of Negro state college, according to regular state procedures, directly to student
10. West Virginia	State board of education through supervisor of Negro schools	1. Application blank 2. Official transcript 3. Statement from institution of satisfactory work	By state treasurer, upon signature of state superintendent to the institution

Source: Reid E. Jackson, "Financial Aid Given by Southern States to Negroes for Out-of-State Study," *Journal of Negro Education* 13, no. 1 (1944): 30–39.

all-White state boards of education, sometimes with input from local HBCU presidents and deans, who were often restricted to being nonvoting members of these commissions and committees reviewing and making selections among Black student applicants.

The dual system states were so committed to the separation of Blacks and Whites in all aspects of life that nine of them cumulatively spent more than $1 million—$1,165,854.92, to be exact—on Negro tuition scholarships between 1921 and 1944. Jackson documents the annual appropriations for this period with data showing a range of allocations, from a low of $10,000 (Arkansas) to a high of $270,000 (Virginia) (see table 2.3).

For example, the state of Maryland allocated $30,000 for the 1938–1939 school year for "scholarships and partial scholarships for negroes."[4] The act permitting this allocation was titled "Interracial Commission" and subtitled "Negro Scholarships." According to the Maryland statute, the Negro Scholarships were available to those who were qualified based on health, character, preparatory education, and ability

> [t]o provide professional or other scholarships for negroes otherwise qualified for admission to the University of Maryland and who cannot obtain desired courses at Morgan or Prince Anne Colleges [two historically Black colleges] for the purposes of securing for such negroes, without additional cost, educational facilities equal to those afforded White students.[5]

Similarly, in 1939, in House Bill No. 255, titled "Appropriations for Institutions of Higher Learning," the Texas legislature allocated $25,000 for "scholarship aid to qualified Negro students" via the state's HBCU, Prairie View Agricultural and Mechanical College (now university) for the term of August 31, 1940, to August 31, 1941. (For comparison, that same state budget allocated $38,942.00 for Prairie View's general maintenance and equipment—and $119,668 for maintenance and equipment at the University of Texas). Texas also required that to obtain this aid, the Black students must be academically qualified, have been a state resident for more than eight years, and be chosen by an all-White selection committee composed of the deans of the all-White graduate schools at A&M College (now Texas A&M University), the University of Texas, and Sam Houston State Teachers College.[6]

Over a one-year period in the early 1940s, Maryland supported 95 Black graduate students and Virginia supported 155. Over a four-year period,

TABLE 2.3 Cumulative Negro Tuition Scholarship Allocations in Ten Segregated States, 1921–1943

STATE	NEGRO TUITION SCHOLARSHIP ALLOCATION
Arkansas	$10,000
Kentucky	$67,000
Maryland	$220,000
Missouri	$220,000
North Carolina	$97,228.92
Oklahoma	$91,626
Texas	$150,000
Virginia	$270,000
West Virginia	$40,000
Total	**$1,165,854.92**

Source: Reid E. Jackson, "Financial Aid Given by Southern States to Negroes for Out-of-State Study," *Journal of Negro Education* 13, no. 1 (1944): 30–39.

Texas supported 145. These numbers grew exponentially over the next few decades. In Georgia alone, the number of Black educator recipients of the out-of-state scholarships grew from 5 in 1944 to 1,790 in 1950.

Not only did the budget allocation for the tuition programs vary by state, but the individual award amounts varied by fields of study. In Maryland, a single-semester tuition scholarship for study in education was $15.00, compared with $266.50 for the social sciences. In Virginia, it was $226.05 for education and $18.00 for French.[7] As a point of reference, during the 1938–1939 academic year, tuition at Columbia University for a graduate student in education was approximately $150.00 per semester.

BLACK EDUCATORS: MORE QUALIFIED THAN WHITE EDUCATORS

In these dual-system settings, Black people were taxpaying citizens of their home states but barred by state law from attending their state's White-restricted colleges and universities. Generations of Black citizens played by the rules—convoluted, imposing, and insulting as they were—and trekked to the Northeast, the Midwest, and even west to California to earn master's and doctoral degrees, so that they could return to their home states in the South to serve as principals and teachers.

Ironically, this arrangement had a decidedly positive impact on the academic credentialing of Blacks in the southern states, particularly principals and teachers. Unable to pursue graduate education at many HBCUs because of these institutions' focus on undergraduate education, and locked out of their state's White-reserved segregated universities, Blacks seeking graduate degrees followed the rules and enrolled in an array of northern universities, both public and private. Often, these institutions were academically superior to the Whites-only schools in Black students' home states.

Jackson found that in three segregated states (Maryland, Texas, and Virginia) in the 1940s, the majority of tuition grants supported students in education (220 students), medicine (68 students), and social work. The preference for graduate work in education appeared to be tied to Black teachers' "desire for professional improvement or else the compelling necessity of extended study, in order to upgrade teachers' certificates."[8]

Most of the era's Black graduate and professional students living in Maryland, Texas, and Virginia chose to attend (in order of preference) Columbia University, Howard University, the University of Michigan, Meharry Medical College, and New York University. They likely selected these institutions because they had national reputations, a track record of successfully graduating Black students in graduate and professional fields, and urban locations in cities with supportive and cohesive Black communities, as well as some Whites with "liberal thinking towards the Negro."[9]

In fact, a small number of Black students had been a consistent presence at elite schools such as Harvard, Yale, Columbia, and Oberlin since before the Civil War.[10] During the Jim Crow–era academic pilgrimages of the 1900s, the trail of Black principals and teachers headed north clustered at Columbia University, the University of Chicago, the University of Pennsylvania, New York University, the University of Michigan, The Ohio State University, and Iowa State University. Here they earned master's and doctoral degrees in educational administration and other fields. Significantly, these educators' treks were not an exodus; rather, they were migrations that had them return to the South to serve in segregated Black schools.

In her testimony before the Senate Select Committee about this practice, Dr. Bettie M. Smith responded to a query from Senator Walter Mondale (D-SD), the committee chairperson, about how she earned her PhD at New York University. "In many instances the Black principal is better prepared, because we were not privileged to attend our state universities and were given grants by the [state] Department of Education to attend universities outside of our state," Dr. Smith explained. "Therefore, most of us took advantage of this grant and received our advanced degrees in the eastern universities."[11]

At the time of her testimony, Dr. Smith had been fired and replaced by a White male with a master's degree from the University of Georgia and only three years' experience. Smith held a bachelor's degree from an HBCU, Tennessee Agricultural and Industrial University (now Tennessee State University), and master's and doctoral degrees from New York University. She had fifteen years of administrative experience.

High school principal O. F. Frazier, like Dr. Smith, held a master's degree in school administration from a highly ranked northeastern university (Teachers College of Columbia University in New York City); he was removed from the principalship of all-Black Conecuh County Training School (later Thurgood Marshall High School) in Evergreen, Alabama, in June 1970 and replaced by a White male. Frazier was reassigned as a Title I Program Coordinator of Visual Aids, a position he described as "created especially for me to prevent assigning me to a principalship."[12] Similarly, John Douglas Fredd of Centreville, Alabama, held a bachelor's degree from the HBCU Alabama Agricultural and Mechanical College (now Alabama A&M) and a master's degree from Teachers College of Columbia University. Fredd had twenty-three years of experience as a teacher, principal, and supervising principal—but on May 25, 1970, he received a letter from his district superintendent bluntly blaming the desegregation mandate for his pending dismissal: "Under the provisions of the court order, your job as principal of Davidson School has been abolished. By order of the Board of Education, I am notifying you that your contract will not be renewed for the school term 1970–1971."[13]

The stellar training and credentials earned by Smith, Frazier, and Fredd were not exceptions; rather, they were the rule for Black principals since at least the early 1900s. Black graduates of HBCUs had a long association with elite northeastern colleges and universities. Horace Mann Bond reported that the Teachers College of Columbia University awarded 144 doctoral degrees to graduates of Black colleges between 1930 and 1960. Bond, who became president of two HBCUs, Fort Valley State University and Lincoln University, had earned his undergraduate degree from Lincoln University, a Pennsylvania HBCU, and gone on to earn master's and doctoral degrees from the University of Chicago. His dissertation on Black education in Alabama won the prestigious Rosenberger prize in 1936.

Ivy League degrees or not, White superintendents and principals throughout border and southern states attacked the competence of Black principals and teachers as a way to justify illegal firings and demotions and the exponential increase in the hiring of White educators. When asked to explain the legions of dismissals of Blacks, John Mize, director of the Division of Administrative Leadership Services in the Georgia State Department of Education, gave this patently untrue answer: "We were lax about the quality of our Black teachers before desegregation. Now we are paying the price and having to clean house, which is why more Blacks have been fired in the last 12 months."[14]

The facts did not support Mize's assertion, at least if "quality" is measured by objective standards such as documented academic credentials earned from top universities and measurable years of experience as professional educators. State by state, reports confirmed that White principals and teachers had minimal credentials and fewer years of professional experience than Black educators, though they were being hired to replace Blacks. According to the Maryland State Department of Education study, *A Comparison of Certificate and Degree Status of Maryland Principals by Race for the School Year 1968–1969*, Black principals were more likely to have a master's degree (63.6 percent), compared with 59.9 percent of Whites. Additionally, Black principals were more likely to hold advanced certifications at the highest (most desirable) levels of certification. Slightly more than 80 percent (80.7 percent) of Black principals held advanced certification, compared with 71.0 percent of White principals. White principals were twice as likely (at 20.9 percent) to be only provisionally certified as their Black peers, only 10.8 percent of whom held this lowest level of licensure. Nineteen White principals in Maryland were without a bachelor's degree, while there were no Black principals in this category.[15] The report concluded, "The one factor in determining the appointment of principals is the racial factor. Since Black principals tend to be more qualified than White principals with respect to degree and certification status, it is necessary for those who appoint principals to provide data that would explain why the discrepancy between Black and White principals [exists]."[16] The Maryland Department of Education acknowledged and warned that the discriminatory treatment of Black principals must cease: "Until there is a conscious and concerted effort on the part of school authorities to make the best and most efficient use of all qualified personnel; until true competence rather than race is the basis for selection and assignment, the future of the Black principal is dismal indeed."[17]

Maryland was not the only state to confirm the superior credentials of Black principals. A 1971 report, *Mississippi Counties Where All Black Secondary Principals Have Been Diminished,* listed fifty counties that had removed all Black high school principals. The report found that "in many instances, the Black principals fired or demoted had degrees in school supervision and administration from universities whose status is superior to that of the Whites who replaced them. Some Black principals were succeeded by principals who did not have the master's degree, as did the Black principals. We are forced to conclude, on the basis of the data presented, that racial factors are operating which favor Whites in the appointment of principals."[18]

J. K. Haynes, executive secretary of the Louisiana Education Association, used his time in the hearings to discuss the debilitating pattern of assumptions operating behind principal appointments. These tacit agreements resulted in Louisiana's elimination of sixty-eight Black principals—and the addition of sixty-eight White principals—between 1968 and 1970, during the height of school desegregation. "In nearly every instance in the unitary school system," Haynes said, "the assumption is that a Black principal, regardless of his qualifications, is not to serve as administrator in an integrated school."[19]

C. C. Bond, assistant superintendent of Chattanooga Public Schools in Tennessee, noted the same race-based trend in his report to the committee, based on his experience serving on national and regional boards and hearing reports from a number of "responsible educators, both Black and White." In his report to the committee, *The Status of Black Principals during the Process of Desegregation in Tennessee,* Bond testified, "I can personally attest to the fact that many of the Black educators who have had these traumatic experiences during the process of desegregation are first-rate educators, possessing a high degree of training, experience, and commitment. In some instances, they were superior to their White counterparts, who were less well-prepared academically, with far less experience. The over-riding criterion seems to have been race."[20]

THE NAACP AND BLACK TEACHERS ASSOCIATIONS COLLABORATE IN THE FIGHT

Black educators fought against this discriminatory and illegal treatment through their major professional organization, the American Teachers Association (ATA). This association existed because of Black educators' sense of professional agency and because membership in the National Education Association (NEA), the American Federation of Teachers (AFT), and the National Association of Secondary School Principals (NASSP) was initially restricted to Whites (although later opened to Blacks as a result of their activism and strategic collaboration).

In 1904, a call by J. R. E. Lee of Tuskegee Institute in Alabama resulted in the founding of the National Association of Teachers in Colored Schools (NATCS). State and local Black teachers' associations already existed across the nation, the earliest having been established in Springfield, Ohio, in 1861. Such associations were largely located in the South, but no national body united all the groups. Once founded, NATCS grew rapidly. By 1933, some fifteen thousand Black teachers, principals, and supervisors were members. Incorporated in Washington, DC, with a headquarters Montgomery, Alabama, NATCS was heavily influenced by Howard University and by Miner Teachers College, both located in Washington. Howard University scholars and alumni Alain Locke, Nannie Helen Burroughs, Lucy Slowe, and Garnet Wilkerson signed the organization's original letter of incorporation. After being inspired by the "new Negro movement," Dr. Willa Carter Burch, a Howard University alumna, Miner Teachers College professor, and administrator at Dunbar High School in Washington, DC, led the charge during a national convention in 1937 to change NATCS's name to the racially neutral American Teachers Association (ATA).[21]

ATA's presidents were an academically credentialed, professionally accomplished, and activist group. They mirrored the distinguished achievements of the organization's rank-and-file members, who were also exceptionally credentialed advocates (especially in light of the nation's racially restrictive and hostile social climate) for equal educational opportunity. More than half of the ATA presidents who held office between 1910 and 1951 had earned undergraduate or graduate degrees (some as early as the 1800s) from top-ranked institutions such as Brown University, Columbia University, Harvard University, the University of Chicago, the University of Pennsylvania, and New York University. Table 2.4 lists ATA presidents and their credentials for the period of 1910 through 1951.

State chapters of the ATA were enlisted to engage educators nationally and locally. This engagement became especially critical during the post-*Brown* integration years. Officers of the all-Black Florida State Teachers Association

TABLE 2.4 ATA presidents' years of service and academic credentials, 1910–1951

ATA PRESIDENT	YEARS OF SERVICE	ACADEMIC CREDENTIALS
William Taylor Burwell Williams	1910–1913	1893, Phillips Academy (Andover, MA) 1897, Harvard University
Matthew Winfred Dogan	1912–1914	1886, AB, Rust College
Nathan Benjamin Young	1914–1915	1888, BA, Oberlin College
John Hope	1915–1916	1894, BA, Brown University
John M. Gandy	1911–1920	1898, BA, Fisk University 1901, MA, Fisk University
Mary McLeod Bethune	1923–1924	1893, BA, Scotia College
William A. Robinson	1926–1927	1913, BA, Atlanta University 1924, MA, Columbia University
John W. Davis	1928–1929	BA, Morehouse College
Mordecai Wyatt Johnson	1929–1930	BA, Morehouse College AB, University of Chicago
Fannie C. Williams	1930–1931	1920, BA and Bachelor of Pedagogy degrees, Michigan State College (now Michigan State University)
Harper Councill Trenholm	1931–1932	1920, AB, Morehouse College 1921, PhB with special honors, University of Chicago 1925, MA, University of Chicago
Garnet C. Wilkerson	1934–1935	1898, BA, Howard University MA, University of Pennsylvania
Rufus Early Clement	1935–1936	BA, Livingstone College 1930, PhD, Northwestern University

Source: Compiled from Al-Tony Gilmore, *All the People: NEA's Legacy of Inclusion and Its Minority Presidents* (Washington, DC: NEA, 2008).

(FSTA), Alabama State Teachers Association (ASTA), Mississippi Negro Principals Association (MNPA), Georgia Teachers and Education Association (GTEA), and North Carolina Teachers Association (NCTA), among others, submitted numerous statewide reports to civil rights and government agencies detailing the names, credentials, districts, and schools of Black educators who were demoted or fired. These state affiliates also filed court cases. At one point, the NCTA had forty-six cases in court, with eleven more ready to be filed and twenty-two additional ones under investigation. The ASTA, which represented ten thousand Black educators, was successful in intervening as party plaintiff in cases covering one hundred school districts.

Civil rights organizations including the Legal Defense and Educational Fund (now the Legal Defense Fund) of the NAACP, the Commission on Democracy in Education, the Delta Ministry of the National Council of Churches, and the American Friends Service Committee joined forces with ATA state affiliates. With unrelenting precision, Black principals lobbied the NEA to integrate its executive body and membership. The principals then crafted leadership roles for the NEA, the NASSP, and the AFT by providing data, composing reports and testimonies, and vigorously pressing for *amicus curiae* briefs to be written in support of Black principals and teachers. Notably, these educators filed large numbers of lawsuits and engaged in letter-writing campaigns to the US Department of Justice urging investigation of the widespread discriminatory treatment of Black educators and protection of their rights. National professional associations and civil rights organizations found allegations of Black professional incompetence to be untrue and spoke out about this illegal treatment. In a letter dated September 24, 1970, to Senator Walter F. Mondale (chair of the Senate Select Committee), David W. Meade, the executive secretary of the North Carolina Teachers Association, expressed concern about less-qualified Whites replacing Black principals and urged investigation by the DOJ: "In many cases Black principals who are certified and have years of service in the community are being replaced by White principals who have neither the certificate nor the experience in either the position or the community. . . . Our national association sent a letter to the Attorney General's office in August. This letter called the situation to the attention of the Attorney General's office and requested an investigation by the Department of Justice."[22]

Lest anyone believe that the problem of Black principals being demoted, fired, and replaced by unqualified Whites was limited to only a few districts, the NEA and NASSP confirmed a region-wide trend. In their 1970 report outlining the failures and critical consequences of desegregation, a NEA task force found that hundreds of Black educators were being "demoted, dismissed, or pressured into resigning. Blacks are then replaced by Whites who often have fewer qualifications and less experience."[23] In its multistate report, the NASSP linked the pattern of Black school closures to Black principal demotion and the loss of talent: "If [the Black principal's] building is used after desegregation, he may be retained as an assistant to a White principal in the same school in which he was the principal. This is the pattern even when the Negro principal is better qualified in terms of training and experience and is rated 'excellent' by his superiors."[24]

Thomas William George, a NASSP attorney, emphasized the same finding in his statement to the Senate committee: "The common rationale for Black displacement is the assertion of lack of qualifications through inferior academic training. However, several educational leaders and official reports point out that because of special effort required for a Black individual to originally attain the principalship, the credentials of Black principals are not infrequently superior to those of their White counterparts."[25]

BLACK STUDENTS, HOSTILE SCHOOLS—AND NO BLACK EDUCATORS

On December 4, 1970, the US district attorney in Alabama filed a Motion for Supplemental Relief alleging that the Limestone County (Alabama) Board of Education had discriminated against Black principals and teachers. The evidence showed that four Black principals had been demoted, one of whom subsequently left the system. The board filled a vacant principalship with a White principal who was less qualified than the Black principals who had been demoted. In addition, the evidence pointed to a discriminatory hiring policy. Only one Black teacher had been hired in the past two years. By January 4, 1971, the district court had ruled: Limestone County had to remove the less-qualified White principal and fill the position with one of the three Black principals who had been demoted. The court also ordered that the two remaining Black principals who had been demoted be offered principalships before anyone else was hired from outside the system, that all demoted principals receive a salary supplement equal to the compensation they would have received as principals, and that this supplement continue until each was offered a principalship. The court also required that the district submit semiannual reports showing the existence, special requirements, and qualifications of vacancies as well as the name, race, education, certification, experience, and acceptance or rejection of all applicants.[26]

As legions of such stories illustrate, even as the numbers of Black students grew in integrated schools, the desegregation years of 1954 to 1968 proved devastating to Black educational leadership. The treatment of Black educators, especially highly regarded Black principals, "really takes a toll—an immeasurable toll—on the morale of the Black community," testified Dudley

Flood, associate director of the Division of Human Relations in the North Carolina Department of Instruction. "The leader, the link, the recruiter and the symbol is gone."[27] Samuel B. Ethridge, associate secretary of the NEA's Commission on Professional Rights and Responsibilities, also understood that the elimination of Black principals was especially burdensome to the Black community. In his June 16, 1971, letter to committee chair Senator Walter F. Mondale, Ethridge wrote: "The Black principal in most Southern communities is the highest public official in the county. His status in the Black community is relatively much more important than his counterpart in the White community.... This fact was touched on lightly in the written testimony, but it was not underscored in this precise language: '*The Black Principal is the Highest Public Official.*' To downgrade him is to downgrade the Black *community*."[28]

By the time of the Senate hearings in June 1971, some witnesses alleged that the damage was done, and time had run out on rectifying the problem. An editorial from the *Roanoke (Virginia) Tribune* submitted to the Senate committee offered a grim summary:

> A Black administrator with years of experience, certified as the head of an accredited secondary school, represents a continuous educational resource to any school division. The leadership role in the community is now lost. This influence and representation on the policy making level is now diminished.... The authority of the Black administrator, which could represent the final avenue of understanding, guidance, and communication, is now a vanishing reality.[29]

Although the damage continued, it did not dissaude Black educators and their allies from continuing to document what the elimination of entire generations of Black educators meant for the nation's schools, the educational profession, both Black and White children, and the Black community. What did it mean to purge legions of highly credentialed and effective principals and teachers from the nation's schools? What did it mean to have them replaced by less-qualified ones? How would this affect the nation's Black and White schoolchildren?

The elimination of the Black principal constituted "the waste of a significant and tried storehouse of professional talent, training, and experience," according to Dr. Owen Kiernan, NASSP executive secretary. In testifying about what the "deepening crisis" portended for the nation, Kiernan explained the consequences:

> In the principalship were competent and dedicated men and women who could be looked up to, and who could serve as prime examples of what American education could produce. Today, many of these community leaders are no longer in a position to set examples or exercise leadership. In far too many cases, they have been dismissed or transferred, stripped of their leadership role, and reassigned as second-class professionals.[30]

Convinced that principals were examples of "leadership and inspiration," Senator Edward Brooke concluded that their elimination could "only have a disastrous effect not only on the morale of the Black students, but on an entire school system."[31] Chattanooga Public Schools assistant superintendent C. C. Bond highlighted the symbolic power of the Black principal to Black and White children: "The Black child needs a model with which to identify, along with live examples of his own race, in places of prestige and responsibility. This serves to lift his aspirations and to remove the perceptions of inferiority and second-class citizenship. Then, too, it is most significant to our society for White children to have experiences under first-rate Black educational leadership. This will go a long way in changing their perceptions and prejudices about race."[32]

The NEA's *amicus curiae* brief filed on behalf of displaced Black principals in *United States et al. v. State of Georgia et al.* explained that "the public schools in this circuit have absorbed the best trained and most successful members of the Negro race" and that the mistreatment of Black educators would be a "constant reminder to Black students of their own inferior status in desegregated schools." The brief warned that "to the extent that Black educators are mistreated, attitudes of superiority among White children, teachers and parents are reinforced, thus tending to undermine the desegregation process from each direction."[33]

J. C. James, a Federal Executive Fellow at the Brookings Institution, former associate dean of admissions at Howard University, and former chief of the Southern Branch of the Division of Equal Educational Opportunity in the US Office of Education, weighed in with a compelling statement on role modeling by Black principals: "They provided a valuable image for Black kids. At least they would know that there was something to do other than chop cotton for Mr. Charlie, cook in his kitchen, mop his floors, wait on his tables, and perform numerous other menial chores during his lifetime. Black teachers supervised by Black principals provided an image of authority and respectability, and last but not least, a better standard of living than most were accustomed to."[34]

Similarly, in a passionate plea before the Senate Committee, John F. Banks, associate director of secondary education for the Virginia Department of Education, challenged the nation to consider the needs of all of its children as it staffed schools. "All the children of all the people must be our concern," Banks said, "and if these children are to grow and develop in a good climate of cultural aspiration, if they are to develop all of their talents and potentialities, if they are to learn to love, respect and cherish the dignity of all human beings, then we need the unity of all talent and resources and the concerted efforts of all people."[35]

Others worried about the quality of teachers that Black children would be left with in the integrated system. A Louisiana report noted that "invariably it is the best Negro teachers who are transferred to the White schools, while it is felt that the Black schools, where [these schools] remain, get the worst White teachers in exchange."[36] There was also concern that too many White teachers were teaching outside of their fields of certification. A report from the NAACP Education Committee found "there are no Blacks in the system teaching out of their fields of certification. However, in several buildings, White teachers have been and are now teaching in areas in which they are not fully certified."[37] A 1955 *Report on the Department of Teacher Information and Security* found that even Black teachers in rural one-room schools were more credentialed than their White counterparts:

> A teacher in a rural one-room schoolhouse in West Virginia was notified that his contract would not be renewed for the 1953–54 school year. His fourteen Negro grade-school pupils were integrated in the local White elementary school. This man's ability as a teacher and his superior training—he received a BA and a master's degree from accredited colleges—were not questions. Of the five White teachers in the local White elementary school, four are employed on "emergency" certificates issued by the school authorities for employment of teachers who have not completed academic requirements, including a bachelor's degree from an accredited college.[38]

Without representative numbers of excellent Black principals and teachers, concern grew that Black students' aspirations would suffer. According to the report to the Senate committee presented by the GTEA, "The elimination of Black educators must be stopped not only for the welfare of the educators themselves, but also because the continued loss of professional positions will discourage Black students from aspiring to become teachers and other professionals. In addition to their teaching, Black educators are, and must remain, prime examples to Black youth."[39]

Dr. Albert Baxter, a professor at an HBCU, the Arkansas Agricultural, Mechanical and Normal College (now the University of Arkansas at Pine Bluff), testified that "Black young people's belief in the reality of the American dream could not be more dramatically violated than by this displacement" of Black principals.[40] When Black students do not have a safe and inspiring school to attend, they will create alternatives, Dr. Baxter argued. In their testimonies, both Dr. Baxter and John Banks described the discouragement felt by Black students in one Arkansas community and discussed the self-protective actions they took. Rather than be abused and humiliated in desegregated schools, this "group of 300" established their own school, "the Soul Institute." The two men described the community in the Senate hearings:

SENATOR MONDALE: What is the impact upon the Black school child in your judgment of this phenomenon of the demotion of Black principals? How does the Black child respond to that? Mr. Banks, would you care to respond to that question?

MR. BANKS: Yes, I think that is possibly the most important and most sensitive area of that problem . . . the most tragic and important concern is what he [the principal] is going to do with the Black youngsters. What will his [the student's] aspirations be, the hope in the future, the motivations, the challenges that are part of their daily lives. Your Black youngster is left hopeless, frustrated, discouraged and they are asking questions, they are asking questions. What is the future? What does education offer to me?

DR. BAXTER: Senator, may I cite one example?

MR. MONDALE: Yes, sir.

DR. BAXTER: In Earle, Arkansas, the district has a pupil population of approximately 1,500, of which 900 are Black and 600 are White. When the school was unitized last year, after about a month of

> schooling 300 Blacks refused to go to school. They stated they were being discriminated against far more effectively than they had ever been in the segregated schools. . . . They have since established what is called "the Soul Institute" (the 300 who are not going to school) in a small, ragged building in Earle and in the church house. The high school students attend the Soul Institute, a small building near a funeral parlor. The elementary children go to school at the church house. They will not go back to school, so they say, until some justice has been brought to bear upon this particular problem. They contend that the education they are getting at "the Soul Institute" is inadequate, but it is superior to the education that they were receiving in [integrated] Earle High School.[41]

In short, with Black educators being held fast in the vise-grip of desegregation, Black students were left particularly vulnerable and subject to mistreatment by White principals, teachers, and students. In many ways, the expulsion of Black principals and teachers took away Black students' means to achieve an education. NEA investigators found schools where White principals operated separate bell systems for Black and White students and classrooms where White teachers called students racial names, placed them in the back of the classroom, turned their backs to them during instructional time, and ruined their homework and project assignments.[42]

In these schools, White principals did not always protect Black students or lend a hand when they were brutalized. LaVon Wright Bracey recounted the hope and terrorism of her days as a senior at Gainesville High School in Florida. Her father, the Reverend Thomas A. Wright, was president of the local NAACP chapter and filed suit against the Alachua County Board of Public Instruction for maintaining segregated schools. At the time of the suit, eleven of the county's schools were segregated, including the all-Black Lincoln High School and the all-White Gainesville High School. After winning the lawsuit in 1964, the Reverend Wright attempted to recruit Black parents to register their children at Gainesville High. Overwhelmingly, parents thought it too dangerous. Wright found only two volunteers, one for the sophomore class and one for the junior class, but no one for the senior class of the desegregating White high school.

During that time, Bracey remembers that she could not sleep because she "could only see my dad's disappointed face each time I closed my eyes." So one morning, she decided to remedy her dad's disillusionment. The morning after a disappointing recruitment campaign, she rushed to greet him and proclaimed, "Here I am, send me. I'll go to the White school." As the daughter of a preacher, Bracey's zeal may have been inspired by the biblical story of Jeremiah as well as her empathy for her father's cause. "Are you sure?" her father asked. "Yes," she responded. "I must promote the cause. I will sacrifice my twelfth-grade year to open the door of opportunity for other black students for generations to come." Once at school, she was faced with physical and mental brutality and with a White school principal unwilling to help her. In order to pass through the schoolhouse door, she had to marshal unusual bravery each day before and after being attacked by a mob of White teenage boys.

> On that first day, Dad drove me to school, followed by a Gainesville police car. I received stares and was called all kinds of nigger. No one spoke to me. No one sat near me. I could expect each day to have some White male or female spit on me and call me nigger. I began to hate. The thought of looking at someone with White skin made me sick. After about a month at the school, a group of White boys jumped me and beat me bloody. No one offered any assistance. The principal said, 'How do I know that you did not come to school bloody from your home? I did not see anyone mistreat you.'[43]

In 1965, LaVon Wright became the first Black student to graduate from Gainesville High School. She explained what she thought and felt as a young teenage girl in those days after the assault: "I stayed home for three days, pondering what to do. I refused to allow them to win. I returned. The year was long, silent, unhappy. The scars are still there."

Later, she graduated from Fisk University, became a wife and mother, and earned a doctorate in education from the University of Florida. Even with the terrors of her senior year of high school well behind her, at sixty years old, she still described 1964 as "the worst year of my life" and reflected that it was a spiritual struggle to heal "after experiencing so much resistance, evil, and hatred."[44]

Other dangerous and new patterns of racial segregation came into existence in the newly desegregated districts and schools. Desegregated schools contained segregated classes. And segregation could be found within classrooms, too. All of this ugly resistance exacted a sad and heavy toll on Black children. The NEA report concluded, "An entire report could be written describing the kinds of mistreatment to which Black students are subjected, how they have reacted, and the brutal impact of continuing discrimination on self-worth and ability to learn."[45]

The interests and identities of Black students were submerged under the intense pressure to desegregate schools and to maintain White control of them. Of 322 districts the NEA reviewed, only 83 were found to have trophies won by Black students on display at the desegregated high school, while 206 districts displayed trophies won by Whites. The NEA report gave this evocative account: "Left behind to be stored, scattered or abandoned are trophies, pictures, plaques and every symbol of Black identity, of Black students' achievements and of their school's history."[46] In those rare instances when district leadership adopted racially sensitive curricular materials, White parents' opposition was yielded to, according to the NEA report: "In another school system, new multiethnic textbooks were purchased at the beginning of the 1969–70 school year. The books were withdrawn because White parents threatened to burn them unless the school system discarded them." In this setting, Black students had little chance of identifying with their "desegregated school." Black symbols of pride were "destroyed and derogated."[47]

How could the nation's schools teach democratic ideals and model equal opportunity, while racially discriminating in the hiring, assignment, and promotion of school personnel? School leadership had to be integrated if desegregation was to mean anything for the nation and its schoolchildren. The writer John Oliver Killens charged:

> In "integrated" schools, too many of the symbols of authority are White.... If integration is to have any meaning for Black children, integration must be achieved at the level of authority as well as at the student body. I mean Black and White kids must experience some Black authority. How can there be incentive without example? ... This distorted image of the Negro has its negative effect on children too. It gives them a distorted image of this earth and of human potential and ill equips them to live in a world three-quarters of which is colored and fast becoming independent and free.[48]

A host of legal decisions affirmed that Black students had a right to desegregated faculties and that this right could not be circumvented by displacing Black educators (*Bradley v. School Board*, 382 US 103, 1965; *Rogers v. Paul*,

382 US 198, 1965; *United States v. Jefferson*, supra, 372F.2d at 884 85). Yet the impact of the decimation of Black principals and teachers could not be fully captured by a body count, astounding though it was. The courts concluded that mistreatment of Black educators and their absence in desegregated schools was a "constant reminder to Black students of their own inferior status in desegregated schools" and "dull[ed] the motivation of Black children." This illegal and discriminatory treatment also reinforced erroneous "attitudes of superiority" among Whites. The result was a clear and deliberate undermining of the desegregation process.[49] Reversing the negative trend was viewed as critical to school desegregation and ensuring no harm come to students as a result of their schooling.

THE ECONOMIC IMPACT OF BLACK PRINCIPAL AND TEACHER JOB LOSS

Even outside of desegregating schools, the impact of decimation was felt by Black educators, community members, and students in public schools and colleges. While the nation wrestled with the educational, political, and social meaning of school desegregation, the economic impact of job loss in the education professions proved catastrophic for the Black community. Dr. J. C. James wrote about the damage in an article, "The Black Principal: Another Vanishing American," published in the September 26, 1970, issue of the *New Republic* magazine. Dr. James described the educational field as a prominent upward mobility strategy chosen by Blacks:

> Traditionally, more Black college graduates have gone into teaching than any other profession or vocation. Teaching in the Negro schools of the South offered the largest job market for college and university-trained Negroes, as well as the only field where there was an opportunity for unlimited advancement within the system. They could be teachers, principals and supervisors of other Blacks in local district. . . . In the communities where they lived and worked, especially in the small towns and rural counties, they were the only educated Blacks, and as a group formed the largest Negro middle-class—middle class not only in terms of economics but in total outlook as well.[50]

What was the damage to the Black middle class when Black principals lost their jobs? One analysis of thirty north Georgia school systems estimated that in these districts alone, the cost borne by the Black community began at $1.75 million a year and climbed from there "due to the number of principals and teachers already lost to the profession; if the trend continues, it would mean a loss of nearly $3 million dollars over the next five years. It should be kept in mind that these are relatively small systems. The larger systems are in the middle and southern part of the state where the loss would be considerably greater."[51]

By 1975, a total of 2,235 Black principalships had been lost. An additional 5,368 Black principals would need to be hired to reach parity with White principal hires. Black teacher job loss between 1954 and 1974 is estimated at nearly 39,386 jobs. Estimates by Samuel Ethridge and Boyd Bosma calculate the loss in teacher salary income to African American communities in the seventeen southern states for 1970–1971 alone at $240 million.[52] This figure would increase by an additional $80 million were Black principals' salaries included.

The Report on the Employment Patterns of Principals, by Race, 1954–1968, submitted to the Senate Select Committee by the Maryland State Department of Education, included this grim assessment: "School desegregation has meant the loss of principalships [for Blacks] and a resultant closing of the door on opportunities for professional advancement. . . . Until there is an increase in the number of Black principals in those systems which offer the greatest opportunity for growth, the chances for Black educators to become principals will continue to remain less than in 1954."

Dr. Albert Baxter's testimony before the Senate Select Committee emphasized the same prognosis; in his view, elimination of Black principals constituted a "debilitating influence on educational aspirations in the Black community." As he explained, "For years, positions in teaching and administration represented a real opportunity to upwardly mobile aspiring young Blacks. This was especially true in the South. If they are now to be denied one more profession offering policymaking opportunities and social status, the effect is bound to be damaging."[53]

Perhaps most important was the Black principal's role in recruiting and employing Black teachers. Citing the increasingly expansive role of school principals, the NEA a*micus curiae* brief on behalf of displaced Black principals in Georgia stated:

> Traditionally, the principal has had a very influential role in the hiring of new teachers and in the evaluation of in-service teachers. Moreover, the

> principal's authority in this regard has been increasing in recent years. He is the administrative official nearest to the classroom, and understandably, superintendents and school boards often defer or at least give substantial weight to the recommendations of principals in hiring and retaining teachers. The Black principal, moreover, has played a leading role in the recruitment of Black teachers. . . .
>
> To the extent that Black principals are eliminated, and the complexion of the principal force becomes increasingly White, Black teachers and applicants will become even more vulnerable to racial discrimination. Thus, the elimination of Black principals will complement and reinforce the drive to eliminate Black teachers in the school districts of this Circuit.[54]

The terms and pace of desegregation were being determined unilaterally by Whites; the guiding edict was that Blacks be removed from positions of power and authority. Oddly, promotion could sometimes be as harmful as firing. Black principals "kicked upstairs" often occupied central office positions with no lines of authority and fuzzy job descriptions. In an explanation of this phenomenon, a NASSP multistate report noted, "He [the Black principal] is now in the central office, where he is the highly visible token of desegregation and director or coordinator of federal programs. If not that, he is given some other title completely foreign to all known educational terminology, a desk, a secretary and no specified responsibilities or authority, with a quiet prayer that he will somehow just go away."[55]

These "pseudo-promotions to central office [have] resulted in the loss of visible leaders in the Black community," explained W. Hobart Millsaps, NASSP president, in his letters to Senator Mondale and Jerris Leonard, assistant attorney general in the DOJ.[56] White control of desegregated schools depended on making Blacks powerless to control schools and classrooms. *Brown* might force Black children to sit side by side with White children in classrooms, but Black educators would not lead alongside Whites. They would be integrated in a different manner—and significantly, those who remained would have little power, authority, or policymaking responsibilities. On May 27, 1971, Dr. Gilbert L. Porter, special assistant to the superintendent of Dade County (Florida) Public Schools, penned a letter to the NASSP president expressing concern about the pattern of White-appointed Black leaders. Porter, a graduate of Talladega College (an HBCU) with a master's degree from the University of Michigan and a doctorate from The Ohio

State University, worried that a new breed of Black educational leaders disconnected from the Black community was emerging. "Blacks who are now placed in positions where they cannot be seen; where they are not looked up to as community leaders and respected as such, now are looked down upon both by the young Blacks, and in many cases, even by the older Blacks because they no longer make or help to make policy," Dr. Porter wrote. "Very few Blacks are sitting at the planning tables where strategy is being planned and implemented in moving toward integration."[57]

AUTHENTIC BLACK LEADERSHIP SUCCESSION THWARTED

At least in the old, pre-1970s segregated system, Black leaders were relied on for their knowledge of the community. In some respects, these leaders were left to their own devices to manage what Whites considered second-rate schools, even though the ethic of Black principals and teachers was that "Black schools should exceed White standards, not imitate them."

Though the school facilities they taught in might have been inadequate, the principals and teachers serving in these settings were more often than not thoroughly competent, known for what Vanessa Siddle Walker calls their "unshakeable will," and their insistence that students *could* "do something." Their presence, instructional methods, and ways of being affirmed the mantra "you can make it." Uniformly educated at HBCUs, pre-*Brown* generations of Black principals and teachers were trained and socialized by an exacting group of well-credentialed Black college faculty who themselves had attended segregated elementary and high schools and earned undergraduate degrees from HBCUs. These HBCU professors were among the first Black Americans to earn doctorates (dating back to the early 1900s) in a variety of disciplines from Harvard, Yale, the University of Chicago, the Teachers College of Columbia University, the University of Michigan, and other elite northern universities. Known for their extraordinarily high academic standards, this faculty instilled in students a determination to succeed against the odds. To them (and unbeknownst to Whites), segregation did not mean "separate and equal"; it meant that even without sufficient resources, they would be "separate and better than."

These well-trained, lifelong Black educators "had their own set of beliefs about how the children should be motivated to achieve."[58] Furthermore, they knew from their own lived experiences that "the social conditions required special sensibilities in and out of the classroom."[59] Working successfully in leadership and teaching positions in a segregated society, Black principals and teachers shared specific strategies for negotiating a larger world hostile to Blacks and stood as models for what could and should be accomplished:

> Those men and women believed that education was the only route available by which their students and the community could "advance as a race." . . . The [Hyde County Training School] teachers believed that they had to sustain "a sense of mission" not shared by White educators. They were preparing their students "to contribute to society and to help somebody." They believed that the Black community would depend on their students, and HCTS alumni long remembered the sense of obligation to make a contribution to the community that was instilled in them.[60]

In this context, the HBCU-trained educators experienced HBCUs as far more than quaint sanctuaries of support and caring; they were citadels of excellence, perseverance, and intellectual rigor. HBCU graduates emerged from their institutions forever changed and grateful to their alma mater. On these campuses, even in the deep South, Blacks were safe from the daily insults and violence of White racism. Here, they were immersed in a setting filled with Black people who were models of intellectual authority and leadership. They learned to negotiate an environment that had a high regard for academic excellence; encouraged knowledge of Black history and culture; required precision in speech and writing; stressed daily structure, discipline, and stamina; and mandated weekly religious observation as a basis for moral character and ethical behavior. At the time, these principles were also recognizable in the broader Black community and viewed as enabling an individual to thrive in a racist world intent on curtailing Black lives and success.

HBCU-trained principals and teachers learned and experienced (as students themselves) a consistent doctrine that declared that:

- The school is *the* prized symbol of the community because it is a transformational institution that prepares the student for a meaningful and productive life.
- The principal is a known, consulted, visible, and respected leader in the school and community who ascends to leadership because of

instructional expertise and an ability to maneuver the district's/city's racial and other politics to acquire resources for the school.
- The teacher is a valued and respected community member expected to set high academic standards and model self-determination and service.
- An orderly and highly structured environment is a prerequisite to learning.
- Pupil acquisition of basic academic skills takes precedence over all other school activities.
- Academic tracks are malleable and intended to ensure that no student falls below minimum levels of achievement.
- A teacher's success is measured by students' academic progress.
- Knowledge of Black history and culture is essential.
- Parents are expected to support school goals and methods.[61]

This doctrine enabled *agency*—"a range of purposeful strategies designed to foster Black self-reliance and empowerment and to resist opposition to the education of Black children."[62]

With desegregation, however, came a ruinous equation for Black leadership ascension. In his letter to the NASSP, Dade County's Dr. Porter asserted that "Blacks who know more about their own people than anyone else in the system or community suddenly are not asked for their opinions." He maintained that "Black-trained leadership in many communities today has deteriorated to the lowest ebb that I have seen in my lifetime."[63] Black teachers confirmed Dr. Porter's doubts about the Black principals promoted by Whites to central office posts. These principals were given newly created titles and placed in offices with no history or lines of authority. Unable any longer to provide other Black educators or Black students with formal leadership, mentorship, or protection, these new positions "block [Black educators] from any decision-making authority or even from knowing what the decisions are until they have been publicly announced," concluded a NASSP multistate report summarizing Black teachers' testimonies. White control of desegregated districts and schools was being created and maintained at the expense of Black power and authority:

> The testimony from Black teachers further indicated that there is a widespread mistrust on the part of teachers of Blacks who do obtain such

> "promotions," for it is felt that the only way such posts can be retained is by assuming an attitude of subservience to White school officials. This is not to say that there are no effective Black administrators in central office positions. If such administrators are able to function effectively, however, it is by dint of their own persistence and strength against overwhelming odds."[64]

Black educators' mistrust was also based on the observation that White school boards and superintendents consistently promoted two types of Black professionals to central office positions—those compliant with a White agenda and those co-opted by it. "Testimony indicated, in fact, that the selection of Blacks for promotion to central office posts is commonly based on two apparently opposing criteria: 1) On their qualifications as 'safe Negroes,' who will cause no trouble; and 2) On their reputations as 'militants' whose aggressiveness may be stifled by co-optation into a position of pseudo authority."[65]

If progress was to be made, "something must be done to reshape the attitudes of superintendents and boards toward Negro administrators," observed Samuel B. Ethridge, associate secretary of the NEA's Commission on Professional Rights and Responsibilities. C. C. Bond held a similar opinion: "I think school boards and school superintendents, because of tradition and customs which prevailed under the dual school systems, have not shown the courage and commitment to give bold and imaginative educational leadership in seeing that the Black administrator was treated fairly and justly in the whole process of desegregation. I honestly feel that their attitude is much more negative than the attitudes of many of their White constituents.[66]

Too few local communities were making efforts to "justify integration of the Negro principal into the same system where he already may have many years of highly respected and forceful service," emphasized N. R. Burger, president of the Mississippi Negro Principals Association, in his letter to Charles R. Hilston, NASSP's Director of Field Service. Though Bond was in Tennessee, Burger saw the same dynamic operating with Mississippi's school boards and superintendents, whom he viewed as needing pressure from their local constituents to do the right thing. "I feel that very little can be accomplished in any direct efforts to work with the local boards of trustees and district superintendents," Burger wrote. "[In] other words, they will do as much as local pressure will permit them to do."[67]

G. W. Ellis summed up the plight of demoted, fired, and displaced Black principals from a personal perspective. As "one of the thousands of Black elementary and secondary principals no longer a school principal," he asked, "is the future one of little hope for protection of the Black educator?" After being relieved of his principal's post, Ellis served as director of education for Phi Beta Sigma fraternity. He submitted his *Summary Views Regarding the Effects of Displacement on Black Administrators* to Roland J. Lehker, NASSP's executive secretary. Ellis pondered the hope of desegregation and criticized those setting education policy for the nation and its states. "If desegregation is the hope of American education, why must the Black always suffer the most? Why should people who are not interested in Black people as citizens have the power to control the future of Black folks by educational abuse? I am more than sure that your statistics will bear out that the Black principal is almost eliminated, because the same parties that cried segregation now and forever are in the policy making position.[68]

Jim Crow's white-knuckled grip might be reluctantly loosening to allow passage of Black children through the schoolhouse door. He would, however, send Black principals away with a reminder that the quiet customs governing who would rule were still solidly in place.

3

POSITION POACHING

The Names and Circumstances of Those Purged

> *The South is being chastised because it has consolidated schools and succeeded with integration [and] they have had a tendency to hire White principals.*
>
> —Senator Sam Ervin (D-NC), 1971

> *What is happening in schools . . . is not integration: rather it is disintegration—the near total disintegration of Black authority in every area of the system of public education.*
>
> —NEA Staff Team on School Desegregation in Mississippi

> *The Association will continue to oppose vigorously desegregation plans and practices that result in the systematic displacement or demotion of Black principals and teachers. It urges federal agencies charged with approving and enforcing plans to do the same.*
>
> —NEA *amicus curiae* brief, 1971

EDUCATOR J. S. SINGLETON JR. came to Bertie County, North Carolina, in 1963. Once there, he assumed principalship of Southwestern High School, a newly consolidated high school made up of the former W. S. Etheridge High School of Windsor and the former J. B. Bond High School of Lewiston. As the newly appointed principal, Singleton was responsible for hiring teachers, developing the curriculum, and organizing extracurricular activities. The school's enrollment grew under his administration and the "success of the school was obvious to all persons in the community and all visitors as well," according to Singleton's May 25, 1971, letter to Dr. Roland J. Lehker of the NASSP.[1]

On September 9, 1964, the Bertie County board of education pleasantly surprised Principal Singleton by acknowledging his successful term as principal with a board resolution. It credited Singleton with being responsible for the school "rapidly gaining the reputation as being one of the outstanding high schools in North Carolina" and acknowledged his "organizational ability [that] welded the student body and faculty from two high schools and a widely divergent territory into a well-disciplined and efficient unit." The resolution concluded that Singleton "has at all times distinguished himself through influence, leadership, ability and fairness" and had "performed his duties as principal of the Southwestern High School in such as manner as to command the highest confidence as a public servant."

According to Singleton, "Everything continued at a normal pace of progress until the court-ordered integration" in 1968. Shortly thereafter, he was demoted to a junior high school principalship, while a White male teacher with no administrative experience and without principal certification was appointed principal of Southwestern, the 1,030-student school Singleton had led for five years. Singleton had earned his principal certification and a master's degree in 1958, but the White male who replaced him as principal had to go back to school after his appointment to study for the principal's certificate. Subsequently, Singleton was fired—after the county superintendent charged that he was incompetent. In a letter to the NASSP entered into testimony before the Senate Select Committee, Singleton alleged that despite his excellent performance as principal of a senior high school, he was ultimately fired because of racist trends in principal appointments:

> During the first year of integration, I was told by the superintendent that his friends had gone against him because he had retained me as principal instead of making the newly assigned White assistant principal the top administrator of the school. The assistant later resigned to accept a position at the private segregated academy in Bertie County as principal. The superintendent had suggested that the assistant have full authority and that I teach him the orderly operation and responsibilities of the principalship.
>
> The entire situation is summarized in the fact that my services were unquestionably satisfactory in Bertie County as principal of a senior high school, until the court-ordered integration, and a scapegoat measure had to be found to meet the current trends regarding reorganization.[2]

After his dismissal from his lifelong career, Singleton was not hired by any district in North Carolina schools for the school year 1970–1971. By May 1971, he was selling Amway products, with profits he described as "very meager."[3]

In another egregious example of racist pressure, death threats provoked the resignation of Jefferson Snipes of Swans Quarter, North Carolina. Snipes notified the district superintendent after he was threatened "with bodily harm or death" by two White male parents because he disciplined their sons for classroom misconduct. After apprising the superintendent of the threats, Snipes reported that the superintendent suggested that he resign "because those parents were 'pretty bad persons' and would probably harm him."[4]

In Starkville, Mississippi, the circumstances surrounding Creed Buck's dismissal pushed against old southern codes about "knowing your place" and other baseless myths. Buck had ten years of experience as a principal in the Starkville school system and served as chair of the Special Problems Committee for the local Black teachers' association. In this role, he protested the district's post-desegregation requirement to have currently serving teachers take the Graduate Record Exam (GRE) and meet a cutoff score set by an all-White school board. After shaking the hand of a White female teacher at his school, Buck was criticized by the superintendent and told that he was not fit for teaching in an integrated school. The superintendent asked Buck for a resignation letter, which he refused to provide. The superintendent then called a special principals' meeting and announced that Creed Buck had resigned.

There were many more testimonies before the Senate Committee—short but equally troubling. In Concordia Parish, Louisiana, Homer P. Williams was demoted from principal to the position of an attendance officer and then later to teacher. His salary was reduced. Despite the terms of his contract, he was notified that he would not be paid during the months of July and August of 1970. In Rome, Georgia, Principal Harold Aldridge was demoted to visiting teacher after serving as principal for twelve years. In Hamilton City, Georgia, Ross Dunn served as principal at two all-Black elementary schools. When the schools were desegregated, a White principal was appointed to serve at both schools, while Dunn was offered a job as an attendance officer. When he refused to accept the new position, he was notified that he would not receive any job, not only in Hamilton City, but anywhere in all of Harris County.

When queried about the challenge of documenting displaced Black educators, one North Carolina human relations specialist who was troubled by the phenomenon quipped, "You can see the tracks, but you can't find the body."[5] He was wrong. State-by-state reports submitted to the Senate listed thousands of well-qualified educators as "displaced Negro principals." The bodies could be and were found. The bodies had names and lives. For example: Nobel Leftwich was dismissed. William Keaton was moved to supervisory principal with no job description. Henry Atkins resigned to prevent demotion. Chester White retired early. Margaret LeGrande was reassigned as an assistant superintendent with no job description.

Some states simply provided the Senate Committee with ledgers listing the Black principals lost to the profession. In Alabama, Arkansas, Texas, and several other states, these experienced educators got one-line acknowledgments for their years of service:

C. H. Bell
St. Elmo, Alabama

Pressely Giles
Yoakum, Texas

W. H. Harris
Goshen, Alabama

A. O. E. Martin
Austin, Texas

James L. Collins
Northpointe, Alabama

Harlan Powell
Corsicana, Texas

Mary Preyer
Eufaula, Alabama

L. F. Chaney
Waco, Texas

Virgil Coleman
Elba, Alabama

Carlean Meriem Fowler
Dallas, Texas

S. A. Meeks
Stuttgart, Arkansas

Gladiola Hughley
Turrell, Arkansas

Willa B. Cole
Camden, Alabama

William Keaton
Arkadelphia, Arkansas

Laron Tucker
Hermitage, Arkansas

Calvin Cunningham
Eudora, Arkansas

W. N. Porter
Erwin, North Carolina

Jewel Butler
Texarkana, Arkansas

Margaret LeGrande
Wilmot, Arkansas

Ruby McMarray
Hensley, Arkansas

E. S. Bishop
Alcorn County, Mississippi

Spencer Durante
Reidsville, North Carolina

Marian Funderburk
Chesterfield, South Carolina

Dr. Ira Bryant
Houston, Texas

C. W. McKinney
Saraland, Alabama

Bruce Buckinsham
Tuscumbia, Alabama

Oresta J. Harper
Midland City, Alabama

Robert T. Beasley
Clanton, Alabama

Johnny Jones
Elmore County, Alabama

James L. Collins
Northport, Alabama

O. J. Brooks
Aliceville, Alabama

Joseph Rowser
Attalla, Alabama

J. W. Beatty
Fayette, Alabama

Walker J. Carroll
Daphne, Alabama

T. W. Lowery
Luverne, Alabama

Mary Preyer
Eufaula, Alabama

Charles Singleton
Manson, North Carolina

W. N. Porter
Lillington, North Carolina

Robert Allen Bracey Jr.
Glen Allen, Virginia

Willie Glaze
Prattville, Alabama

Others were not named, but state reports described their circumstances. In one Louisiana parish, a Black principal was reassigned to teach fourth grade and perform part-time janitorial chores. Another Black principal in Louisiana held a master's degree and had twenty-five years of experience but was reassigned as an "assistant visiting teacher" after being replaced by a White principal. In Rankin County, Mississippi, the principal of a formerly all-Black school (grades 1 through 12) was demoted to administrative assistant for the White principal of the same school, which had been desegregated and reduced to grades 1 through 6. In the same county, a Black principal was replaced by a White male coach with no administrative experience. In Emerson, Arkansas, one principal was made a study hall keeper, and another was made a supervisor of vocational programs. In Georgia, all of the dismissed principals possessed certification and all but one held a master's degree. In Cairo, Georgia, "a principalship position held by a Negro in an all-Negro school has been taken away from Negroes and given to a White person. So have seven teaching positions." In Decatur, Georgia, the principal of Trinity High School was pushed out after serving as principal for fifteen years; he subsequently left education altogether to assume a job in another field.[6]

Other statewide accounts provided a sterile, numerical snapshot of the damage. In his report *Assignment of Black Principals Resulting from the Desegregation of Schools*, Dr. J. C. James, associate director for secondary education in the Virginia State Department of Education, tallied the impact of desegregation on the ranks of Black principals by year and by each Virginia county and city. For the year 1966, James recorded:

COUNTIES
1 general supervisor
1 assigned principal in another school division
1 assigned to college staff
3 supervisors of federal programs
1 retired
1 assigned as a visiting teacher
1 retained in reorganization as junior high school principal

CITIES
1 retained in reorganization as elementary school principal
1 assigned principal in another school division
1 assigned to central office
1 supervisor of federal programs[7]

Similar patterns persisted throughout the state of Florida as well, reported Dr. Gilbert L. Porter, special assistant to the superintendent of Dade County Public Schools and Director of School Board Offices. Dr. Porter described one county where "a White principal was placed over the Negro principal without any explanation, even though the Negro principal was better prepared academically and was experienced as a senior high school principal, whereas the White principal had only junior high school experience and stated that he would be happy to work as the assistant to the Black principal, rather than to work over him.[8]

An NEA task force investigating incidences of Black principal displacement in Mississippi and Louisiana summarized what its researchers saw across the South: "In many instances, the White person who is named principal of the desegregated high school is less qualified through experience and academic credentials than the Black, whose assignment is to a junior high or elementary school."[9]

At least Jim Crow was consistent. The methods used to purge Black principals from school leadership were remarkably similar to those aimed at Black teachers. In the words of T. W. George, the NASSP attorney at the time, "The result is always certain: the elimination of the Black man as a school instructional leader." Overtly or covertly, gradually or suddenly, "the tragic phenomenon of displacement of Black principals took many forms," emphasized George. Outright dismissal, reassignment, demotion, paper promotions, and loss of power were among the numerous methods used to "effectively remove and humiliate the Black principal."[10] George argued that even though the credentials of Black principals were often superior to those of their White counterparts, the final consequence of removing Black principals was the same: greatly reduced authority and professional status, low visibility, and placement in undefined, clerical, or menial positions.

O. F. Frazier, himself a demoted Black principal, expressed a similar concern in his June 4, 1971, correspondence to Dr. R. J. Lehker of the NASSP:

> The plight of the Black principal in Bibb County as well as in the state of Alabama has passed the critical point. Three years ago, there were more than 300 Black principals in the state of Alabama; today, there are about fifty Black high school principals. In an age of many civil rights advancements, many Black communities have witnessed the abolishment of one of the few positions of community leadership that a Black child could relate and aspire to. Action is needed now to correct this gross injustice to the Black child.[11]

In his testimony before the Senate Select Committee, the NASSP's George described displacement methods and their "tragic consequences not only for the individual professionals but for the entire nation." Outright dismissal resulted in many Black principals being dismissed or pressured into resigning and no longer serving in any administrative capacity. In some instances, they were denied any employment as educators in their city, county, or state, especially if they held offices in the NAACP and/or with Black principal or teacher organizations and fought against illegal mistreatment.

In other instances, as we have seen, principals were reassigned as co-principals, associates, assistants, or similarly subordinate positions. These positions not only constituted a demotion but in most instances were a token offering that included "nonresponsibilities" such a "giving out excuses, 'dealing' with Black students, janitorial work, bus supervision and assignment to menial office locations"—all posts that had "little if any relationship to instructional leadership."[12] Black co-principals, associate principals, or assistant principals were sometimes forced to inhabit office spaces that were barely converted bathrooms and utility closets. In one Mississippi school district, the principal of a formerly all-Black junior high school reportedly was offered a position as principal of a formerly all-White elementary school. He declined the assignment when he learned that his office would be in the basement and that he only would be in charge of buses (not route scheduling) and student tardiness.

DEMOTIONS, PAPER PROMOTIONS, AND SALARY REDUCTIONS

The NEA task force reported on the phenomenon of the co-principal—a new position emerging in desegregating districts. The co-principal title was chameleonic. Black co-principals reported to White co-principals, who always held the decision-making authority:

> The Black co-principal at Okolona High School (Mississippi) is co-principal in name only, disciplining only Black students and keeping records of books, repairs, and buses (but not making bus assignments). This educator was called vice-principal last year, until Blacks complained, and his title was changed. A White counselor was promoted to principal over the Black principal, who has an MA and has been a principal in the system for 15 years. The White principal earned the MA after the appointment. The White principal allegedly told him that he, the White, was the principal, and that he would be willing to confer with the "co-principal" but that he would have the final word.[13]

Rampant personnel demotions accompanied the phaseout of previously all-Black junior and senior high schools, often moving Black high school principals to junior high school or elementary school principalships or the headship of a special education school. The consistent pattern was to demote the Black principal to the lower grade level, with fewer students and often at a lower salary. In most instances, the reduction in status did not immediately result in pay reduction; rather, the trend was demotion during the first year of desegregation, followed by pay reduction in the second year to conform to the reduced responsibilities. More often than not, Black principals were demoted to positions in which they reported to White principals who were typically less qualified.

C. C. Bond of Chattanooga Public Schools documented the pattern in his statewide report about Black principal displacement in Tennessee schools. "In no case has a Black principal been assigned to an all-White secondary school," Bond testified:

> Several, as the enclosed report will indicate, have been assigned as assistants to White principals. In these cases, the Black assistant's responsibility is to run errands, "control" Black students, supervise buses, and other types of menial assignments with no real responsibility for curriculum, staff, or other matters where White students or teachers are involved. Others are serving as directors of federal programs, attendance teachers, social workers, elementary principals, classroom teachers, guidance counselors, and a few have secured positions as their own as college teachers, State Department workers, have retired, or are deceased.[14]

The "paper promotion" constituted another form of removal from the principalship. These "promotions to nowhere," often referred to as being "kicked upstairs" were a widespread method to eliminate Black principals. With titles such as "federal program coordinator," "supervisor of child welfare and attendance," and "assistant," Black principals were transferred into central office positions "out of sight and evidently out of mind, to undefined or ambiguously defined duties."[15] These "dead-end street" posts were often funded through federal grants, and when the funds expired, those in the positions were terminated. N. R Burger, president of the Mississippi Secondary School Principals Association, wrote about Black principals' promotion to newly created central office posts in his June 9, 1971, letter to Dr. Roland Lehker of the NASSP. Burger noted that the number of Black secondary school principals had declined from 168 to 19 during the year 1970–1971. Burger wrote,

> It is a well-known fact that most [Black principals] have been given jobs of coordinators of federal projects, special services and other titles foreign to all known educational terminology. Many of these elevated titles carry with them elevated salaries with no spelled-out responsibilities and particularly with no authority. Most have desks, secretaries, and time on their hands. Some have been made directors of Educational Material Centers, or education warehouses; visiting teachers, counselors, book supervisors, and directors of building and grounds.[16]

Burger concluded the solution to the problem did not lie in determining whether or not the Black principal was a qualified or experienced educational leader. More accurately, he believed that the question to be answered was "whether the White students, teachers and patrons of a school or school district will work under or accept the authority that goes with being a Black principal."[17]

Even in those cases where a Black principal managed to retain the position and title, "actual authority was vested in his White co-principal or supervising principal," according to NASSP attorney George. In his testimony, George cited NEA task force findings that documented how desegregation spawned the creation of new titles for Whites as well as Blacks. These new titles—area principal, supervising principal, curriculum coordinator, and others—were meant to maintain White decision-making authority and maneuver around court mandates for fairness in hiring and promotion. "It is widely believed by Blacks that these newly titled Whites constitute the real authority behind the Black principals, who have been reduced to mere figurehead status," reported the NEA. "Task Force members found no dearth of evidence to support this conclusion."[18]

In several Mississippi districts where Black high schools were retained as the site for the desegregated high school, Black principals did not run the school. Rather, their presence and power were strategically neutralized by another newly created position—the assistant superintendent. The assistant superintendent could be found only in those few schools where Blacks retained the principalship after desegregation. Under these circumstances, the Black principal (in title only) reported to the assistant superintendent, whose office was also located in the school:

> The system has created a new post of assistant superintendent; the primary duties of the assistant superintendent appear to be to run the "integrated" high school, since he has no regular responsibilities for any other school in the system. The Black high school principal meets each morning with the assistant superintendent (who occupies the principal's former office) and receives his directions for the day. The principal's office is a remodeled former girls' lavatory. The assistant principal of the high school is White; and the White school secretary is the wife of the assistant superintendent. It is clear that this principal has no opportunity

> to exercise the responsibilities of that office, surrounded as he is by a White assistant, the former White high school principal as the assistant superintendent, and the assistant superintendent's wife as secretary of the school. [19]

Though the patterns of discrimination might shift, whatever administrative device was used, "the objective and the accomplished fact," was "the retention of White control over every desegregated school," according to the NEA task force's multistate report.[20]

A Florida report concurred with the NEA observations on ways desegregation brought reduction of Black control over Black schools and "integrated" schools:

> Regardless of the years of experience or the kind of training or the production of some Negro principals in the State of Florida, they were generally relegated to a backseat position wherever there was a merger or integration of White students and teachers, especially at the senior high school level. I know of only one situation where White teachers and students were integrated on a 50-50 basis and the Negro administrator was maintained. It has been just a one-way street, with Whites moving into Negro principalships of integrated schools and never the reverse.[21]

More overtly, Black principals were also simply not hired. In his January 14, 1971, memorandum to the Chief State School Officers and School Superintendents (a national organization of state and district superintendents), J. Stanley Pottinger, director of the Office for Civil Rights, wrote that it was impossible to "catalog all forms of discrimination" against Black educators, but described several of the more obvious methods under the categories "hiring, promotions, demotions and dismissals." He warned the chief state officers and district superintendents that avoiding recruitment of educators from historically Black colleges/universities (HBCUs) was an illegal mechanism for eliminating Blacks from the hiring pool. "A school district which focuses its recruitment efforts on teacher training institutions attended predominantly by members of one race while ignoring institutions attended predominantly by members of another race is discriminating in its hiring practices," Pottinger wrote.[22]

BROWN DID NOT MANDATE CLOSING BLACK SCHOOLS

Legally speaking, desegregation did not have to mean the closing of all-Black schools—but it was made into an excuse to do so. Numerous judicial decisions made it clear that closing schools purely for racial reasons was unconstitutional.[23] The Fourth Circuit went even further in *Felder v. Harnett County Board of Education* (1969), when it held inadequate a desegregation plan that proposed to close three Black high schools and assign Black students to predominantly White high schools because "there was no explanation offered as to how the School Board determined upon particular schools for extinction."[24] *Brice v. Landis* (N.D.Cal 1969) held that a school district's desegregation plan was not adequate because it placed the burden of desegregation entirely on Black students and did not show the necessity of closing the Black school. Though the ruling in *Wall v. Stanly County Board of Education* had made it clear that a school system could not displace Black administrators and faculty merely because Black schools were closed or integrated as part of a desegregation plan, the closing of Black schools persisted as the primary method for doing away with Black principals.

At the time that the Supreme Court handed down the *Brown* decision, seventeen border and southern states and the District of Columbia had laws requiring separate schools for Blacks and Whites. A decade after *Brown*, racial apartheid was still intact in the South. Border and southern schools did not begin to desegregate in earnest until the late 1960s and early 1970s, primarily after President Lyndon B. Johnson's administration enforced strict guidelines prohibiting the distribution of federal funds to segregated schools. Under the Civil Rights Act of 1964, school districts were forced to comply with guidelines that outlawed racial discrimination in hiring, banned so-called freedom-of-choice plans that used tax dollars to support White-segregated private schools, and approved busing to achieve racially balanced student bodies.

Even so, compliance with desegregation mandates was left in the hands of local officials and typically occurred on terms advantageous to Whites. In most districts, the terms for desegregation were unilaterally determined by Whites, without the involvement of Black educators, students, or parents. The result, according to Dr. G. W. Ellis, a demoted principal who found a new educational position with a prominent Black fraternity, was that Black educators were "demoted, fired, misassigned, assigned, reassigned, phased down, phased around, phased out, given lower professional status, lower salary, lower visibility, reduced authority, responsibilities undefined, involuntarily transferred, used and misused."[25]

In a press release published March 31, 1970, the NEA asserted that the usual pattern of school desegregation was "one-way involving the transfer of Black students to formerly all-White schools."[26] Black secondary schools were special targets for closure and reorganization. In most cases, this meant a change in the name of the school and a change in the status of the principal. Names of great educators were stripped from the names of Black schools. In Virginia, for example, desegregation meant the closing of Black secondary schools named for nationally or locally esteemed Blacks: Carver-Price in Appomattox; James Solomon Russell in Brunswick; S. C. Abrams in Fluvanna; Thomas C. Walker in Gloucester; Edward W. Wyatt in Greensville; Mary Bethune in Halifax; Georgie Tyler in Isle of Wight; Thomas Hunter in Mathews; George Watkins in New Kent; Robert R. Moton in Prince Edward; J. E. J. Moore in Prince George; James Weldon Johnson in York; and George P. Penix in Hampton. Florida's Dr. Gilbert Porter of Dade County told the committee that the erasure of Black schools and Black principals resulted in a dangerous invisibility. "Schools that have been standing in communities for years, named after outstanding Negroes in our country and in our local communities, are now closed," he said. "This does something to the racial pride of Blacks."[27]

Closing Black schools was the primary method for ridding the system of Black principals. Directly after *Brown*, there was little displacement of Black principals, but as Title VI compliance mandates increased, the NEA received reports from Black teacher associations indicating that displacements were increasing. In late 1969, C. J. Duckworth, executive secretary to the all-Black Mississippi Teachers Association, clarified the link between Black school closures and Black principal firing and demotions in seventeen Mississippi school districts. He wrote in his report to the NEA,

> Alcorn County—the Black high school reduced to a junior high school and the Black principal became a federal projects coordinator; Clarke County—the Black high school reduced to a junior high school and the principal made an elementary principal for remainder of the year, after which he was to be terminated; Clay County—the Black high school reduced to a junior high school with a White principal; . . . Franklin County—a Black elementary

> principal replaced by a White principal; Hancock County—the Black high school phased out and only two of 10 Black teachers remain; Harrison County—a Black junior-senior high school eliminated and the Black principal made supervisor of a material center; . . . Itawamba County—all Black schools and principals eliminated; . . . Prentiss County—Black high schools and principals phased out; . . . Marion County—Black high school principals replaced with Whites.[28]

Desegregated schools did not integrate Black symbols of pride and accomplishment. On the contrary, Whites' symbols were maintained, and Blacks' symbols discarded or denigrated. According to the American Friends Service Committee, the prevailing attitude was that "Whites are keeping what they have but the Blacks can use it."[29] Again, Black children shouldered the assault on Black identity that ensued from White resistance to the law. As the committee's report put it, Black students

> are expected to happily identify with Wade Hampton, Jefferson Davis or Strom Thurmond Schools. One of our monitors told of a Black high school girl ashamed to admit she was a student at Robert E. Lee School . . . In Edgefield, South Carolina, the desegregated school retained the old White school's name, Strom Thurmond High, as well as its colors, the Confederate flag, the team name "Rebels" and the school song "Dixie" . . . And in Anderson County, Black students were suspended from the band when they refused to play "Dixie" and march behind a Confederate flag.[30]

Even modern, well-constructed Black schools were often closed. Such was the case with Gainesville High School in Gainesville, Georgia. Gainesville High was a Black school for seventh-to-twelfth grades in a modern, $1.2 million building about six years old. Its Black principal had led the school for eleven years, was well credentialed (with a bachelor's degree from Fort Valley State University and a master's degree from Columbia University), and had been "rated as one of the most progressive school principals in America . . . recognized as such by educators on the local, state and national scene."[31] A Georgia report about Black principals concluded that the town currently had "two excellent high school programs" and that "either high school plant could be used to educate all the pupils, both Black and White." In the end, however, Gainesville High was placed on the list for possible closure and at the time of the report "the Negro principal [had] not been offered the job as principal of the 'single high school' wherever the two schools combine."[32]

Though segregation too often meant that Black schools were housed in inferior facilities, many Black schools, like Gainesville High School, occupied well-constructed and maintained buildings. Ironically, the investment in building new Black schools was not really intended as an enduring good. Their construction was related to an intricate dance choreographed by border and southern states in which the *Plessey* decision justifying "separate but equal" was used to evade implementation of *Brown*. "At bottom" explains historian David Cecelski, the segregationists "preferred the fiscal costs required to improve the Black schools to racial intermixing and its political costs."[33]

Despite the "separate but equal" clause, border and southern states decidedly did not spend equal amounts on the education of Black children and White children. When funds were expended on Black children at all, at best the ratio tended to be 2:1—for every two dollars spent to educate a White child, one dollar was spent to educate a Black child. For instance, in 1923, Prince George's County, Maryland, spent $77 per White student on secondary education, compared with $14 per student for Blacks. In 1930 in Mecklenburg County, North Carolina, the average expenditure per White student was $44, compared with $14 for Blacks. Of course, this inequity resulted in Black students experiencing weather-worn school buildings lacking heat, hot water, and indoor toilets; shabby, overcrowded classrooms with second-hand texts that had been used, often defaced, and discarded by Whites; and lack of instructional and laboratory equipment for the sciences, home economics, and the industrial arts.

UPENDING THE NARRATIVE ABOUT INFERIOR BLACK SCHOOLS

Historically, the Black community—those who were enslaved, freed, or never enslaved—was accustomed to funding and building schools. Beginning in the 1870s, Black southerners engaged a self-reliant quest to establish schools for their children. Though captured in economic and social conditions that favored their being illiterate and unschooled, Black people "turned inward and attempted to construct and maintain the semblance of a common school system from their own meager resources."[34] Their efforts met with success as Black men and women, northern philanthropists, and southern progressives came together to launch the Rosenwald school building fund in 1914. The initiative was funded by Julius Rosenwald, the Chicago philanthropist and president of Sears, Roebuck & Company, at the urging of Booker T. Washington, the first president of an HBCU, Tuskegee Institute. In 1912, when Washington wrote Rosenwald, he told him that "Many of the places in the South where the schools are now taught are as bad as stables." More than a decade later, a 1924 report on Black schools in Prince George's County by school trustees echoed Washington's complaint: "We doubt if any of the stables of the Laurel racetrack would be permitted for a horse if they were as run down as these two places in which teachers are forced to labor."[35]

The Rosenwald schools proliferated as an alternative to state-financed public education. Most of the funding came from Black people, either through private contributions or public tax funds. As educational historian James D. Anderson asserts, "It was Black southerners' enduring beliefs in universal schooling and their collective social action to achieve it that made possible and sustained the Rosenwald school building program."[36] Black parents and community leaders held school construction fundraising rallies throughout the South, often led by Black principals and teachers. These educators, along with ministers and business owners, initiated building campaigns to recruit fellow citizens and lobby White superintendents and school boards for tax dollars to be allocated. They wrote letters to the Rosenwald Fund and to Booker T. Washington requesting information and guidance. The campaigns resulted in sharecroppers' setting aside patches of land (called "Rosenwald Patches"), which might be sold to raise funds or given as land donations from Black families, where Black men and boys would provide the labor to clear land and erect the school.[37]

Anderson's description of the first Rosenwald-supported school in Tennessee (built in 1915) conveys the Black community's financial commitment to schooling: "This fund-raising campaign was organized by a Black principal who was teaching in 'an old lodge' and his wife . . . The new Fayette County school building would cost $3,500 cash. Black citizens contributed $2,200 of this amount, plus additional resources in labor and materials. The Rosenwald Fund donated $500 and the county public school authorities appropriated $800."[38]

In a five-year period between 1915 and 1920, a single Black principal and his teacher-wife led the construction of twenty Rosenwald schools in Fayette County, Tennessee. By July 1, 1932, in southern states from Maryland to

Texas, Black contributions to school building campaigns totaled $4.7 million. A total of 5,357 Rosenwald schoolhouses, shops, and teacher's homes were erected in 883 counties across fifteen states, with a total cost of $28.4 million. The Rosenwald Fund's donation of $4.4 million during this period led local governments to spend an additional $18.1 million on schools for Blacks, with private local White contributions making up the remaining 4 percent.[39]

While Blacks depended largely on their own resources to build schools, tax dollars—collected from both Black and White citizens—were used to build schools for White children. Under this arrangement, Blacks were essentially "double-taxed" for their schools. Still, Rosenwald school names often reflected the Black community's deep gratitude to the Rosenwald Fund, as well as longstanding community sentiments about the importance of schooling. "Among Alabama's 407 Rosenwald structures, one would find the Booker T. Washington School or the Rough and Ready School, reflecting heroes of the times," writes Rosenwald historian Diane Granat. "But a one-room school built for $300 in Wilcox County, Alabama, says it all: The Godsend Rosenwald School."[40]

Even before *Brown* in 1954, many Rosenwald schools began to vanish as better roads and the use of school buses led to larger, consolidated schools. But others remained in use through the 1960s as southern states continued to resist integration. What was truly lost in the closing of Black segregated schools is still being discovered. What is known is that these institutions built with the land, sweat equity, and money of the Black community were shrines to an educational self-determination that grew out of the community's desire to have its children educated so that they might "have a chance," as one sharecropper put it. When the Rosenwald schools and other segregated Black schools were closed, these closures extinguished tangible, visible evidence that Blacks' commitment to education was "in our blood from way back."[41] Black communities losing their schools were all too aware of what these closures portended. Even in isolated rural locales that had not experienced civil rights activism, Black citizens rallied civil rights organizers to the cause of keeping Black schoolhouse doors open as sites for desegregation. As one community member in Hyde County, North Carolina, charged: "We built the school up there" and "*they* want to take it away."[42]

In the push for educational and social equality, *Brown* made the case that Black schooling was inferior due to disinvestment and underinvestment. This strategy relied on evidence that portrayed segregated Black schools as inferior because of inequalities in facilities, lack of transportation, shorter school terms, and overcrowding. The argument won the case but left an inaccurate imprint on history about the existence of educational excellence in Black segregated schools. The "history of assumed unilateral inferiority" stands in stark contrast to accounts of these schools that analyze more than resource allocation, according to educational historian Vanessa Siddle Walker. "Confining explanations of the education in the schools to descriptions of resources has not adequately explained the kind of education African American teachers, principals, and parents attempted to provide under externally restricted circumstances," Walker writes.[43]

In fact, numerous scholars have provided evidence of educational excellence in segregated Black schools. In their work, these researchers highlight the academic environment and student achievements of a number of Black segregated schools with nationally competitive college-preparatory curriculums. Among these were Paul Lawrence Dunbar High School in Washington, DC, as well as other high schools named for Dunbar in Little Rock, Arkansas, and Baltimore, Maryland; Sumner High School in Kansas City, Kansas; Frederick Douglass High School in Baltimore, Maryland; A. H. Parker High School in Birmingham, Alabama; Herrington High School in Newport News, Virginia; and Crispus Attucks High School in Indianapolis, Indiana—all examples of high-quality Black schools that existed throughout the border and southern states before desegregation.

The Dunbar Story told the story of Washington's Dunbar High School, which had three teachers with PhDs as early as the 1920s. Four of the school's first eight principals were graduates of Oberlin College, and two held degrees from Harvard University. One of the early principals of Dunbar, Mary Patterson, became the first Black woman to earn a college degree in the United States—in 1862.[44] Notably, Carter G. Woodson— the "father of Black History Month" and the second Black man to earn a PhD at Harvard University—was a member of Dunbar High School's faculty, where he taught French, Spanish, English, and history. Woodson earned his PhD in 1912, founded the Association for the Study of Negro Life and History (now the Association for the Study of African American Life and History—ASALH), and authored the *Mis-education of the Negro*, among numerous other books. Anna Julia Cooper— the fourth Black woman to earn a doctorate—served for decades as a principal and teacher at Dunbar High School and also authored several seminal books about education and Black liberation. She earned her PhD in

1925 at the Sorbonne. Woodson and Cooper were illustrative of the caliber of faculty at Dunbar High School as well as in many Black schools across the dual-system South.

Dunbar High had a strong history of academic achievement, having students who earned higher scores on standardized tests than two of the three high schools for Whites in the District of Columbia and routinely sending well-qualified students to elite northeastern universities. This was the case with Mary Gibson Hundley, who graduated *cum laude* from Radcliffe College in 1918. Dunbar High produced the first Blacks to graduate from the US Military Academy at West Point and the US Naval Academy, the first Black federal judge, the first Black general, and the first Black person elected to the US Senate since Reconstruction.[45]

According to a 2011 National Academy of Sciences report describing the history of the District of Columbia Public Schools, Dunbar was among other Black schools in Washington that were distinguished for exceptionally credentialed principals and teachers, a solid history of academic achievement, and students who outperformed White students at two of three DC schools on districtwide examinations. "Despite significant disparities in the resources available to Black and White schools, Washington had some of the highest-quality Black schools in the country during the period of legal segregation," the National Academy report asserted, "Dunbar and other Black schools were staffed by many teachers with excellent credentials during this period."

Sumner High School in Kansas City, Kansas, had a similar reputation. In 1926, the roster of Sumner faculty indicated that 41 percent of the all-Black faculty held master's degrees, including three from the University of Chicago. By 1935, the percentage had grown to 61 percent with master's degrees, including three faculty who had earned master's degrees from the University of Chicago, two from Columbia University, and one from Harvard University.[46] Notably, with the integration of the school's faculty in 1968 to include more White teachers, the percentage of faculty members with a master's degree fell below its 1926 level to 35 percent.

Sumner High School students benefited from this cadre of highly credentialed and effective educators, particularly in science. Students were known for their stellar achievement in regional and national science fair competitions. They placed first and second in the interracial Greater Kansas City Science Fair Competition (which drew students from Kansas City, Kansas, and Kansas City, Missouri) for six consecutive years since the competition began in 1952. Sumner students regularly went on to compete in the National Science Fair; in 1953, Sumner was the only high school to produce a "top girl" winner in the Kansas competition.

GUTTING BLACK SCHOOLS' CURRICULA

Despite the myth of Black schools' inferiority, ample evidence exists to challenge the notion that the predominant curriculum at Black secondary schools in the segregated South was nonacademic and industrial. To the contrary, a 1916 study found that southern Black high schools possessed a "large place given to foreign languages and especially to ancient languages."[47] In 1916, cities in nine states—including Richmond, Danville, Norfolk, Petersburg, and Mount Hermon in Virginia; Chattanooga, Nashville, Knoxville, and Memphis in Tennessee; San Antonio, Houston, Fort Worth, Dallas, Beaumont, Temple, Dennison, and Palestine in Texas; Louisville, Paris, Frankfort, Bowling Green, Owensboro, Paducah, and Lexington in Kentucky; Birmingham, Alabama; Little Rock, Arkansas; Baltimore, Maryland; St. Louis, Missouri; and Kansas City, Kansas—all had Black high schools that emphasized the classical liberal arts curriculum, "where many required their students to take Greek, and nearly all made Latin the central subject."[48] Black schools offered college preparatory courses in history, mathematics, physics, chemistry, and English. For decades, Black principals and teachers had clearly oriented the high school curriculum toward college preparatory work.[49] Even in those high schools known as "training schools," more often than not home economics, agriculture classes, and other industrial arts courses were electives, rather than the standard curriculum. In his review of the 1940 class of Hyde County Training School, Cecelski found that of the fifteen HCTS graduates in 1940, "ten had career goals that required at least some college education. Five graduates planned to become trained nurses; three teachers; one a physician; and one a pastor."[50]

In some cases, all-Black schools had curricular offerings such as advanced mathematics, Greek and Latin, and Black cultural history that White schools did not, as was the case with Caswell County Training School in Arkansas.[51] In too many instances, Black principals and teachers had to fight White school board authorities to add advanced courses to their curricula. Foster describes one teacher's struggle to lead this charge. "I often wonder if White folks really want Black kids to be successful," the teacher said. "I started the first advanced math class in Chatham County; this was at Horton, the all-Black, segregated school. The advanced math class was a course where they got beyond geometry and algebra two. But when the county school officials found out what they were doing, they blocked the course. They cut it out until the White school could establish the course and catch up with us. That's how determined the White folks were to be better than we were."[52]

Anderson posited that the existence of HBCUs in southern communities supported the adoption of the classical liberal curriculum at segregated Black secondary schools. These institutions also encouraged the higher education aspirations of Black high school students and short-circuited efforts to focus their education exclusively on industrial training.[53] Excellent or not, however, Black schools were subject to immediate closure as desegregation marched slowly across the border and southern states. As Dr. Gilbert Porter wryly observed, "The geographical location of Black senior high schools, the physical plants in general, and the program offerings, while good enough for Black children, suddenly became obsolete when being considered for integration of White students and teachers. No doubt this had a psychological impact on who would man these schools."[54]

Southern Blacks had a "cultural orientation toward learning and self-improvement" and a muscular history of fighting repressive efforts that limited and misdirected their access to public schools.[55] Despite much progress, generations would continue to struggle to exert control over how desegregated schools would educate their children, now that Jim Crow was relentlessly expelling an entire generation of the best-educated, most visible, and most effective voices in any Black community—its principals and teachers—from its public schools.

4

LITIGATING JIM CROW DESEGREGATION

The Struggle to End the Decimation

> *Black children are not equal to White children and Black teachers are not as good as White teachers. Now goddamn it, that happens to be the truth. So why the hell do you [buck?] against the truth. Isn't that the problem? Now you can't tell them [Black people] that. That's the problem.*
>
> —President Richard M. Nixon
> March 14, 1972, taped conversation
> in the Oval Office with staff and cabinet members[1]

> *The elimination of the Black principal is a disaster caused by the educational power structure (local, state and federal).*
>
> —N. R. Burger, President
> Mississippi Secondary School Principals Association

By 1970, the NAACP Legal Defense and Educational Fund (LDF), spurred by Black teachers associations, had succeeded in the campaign to mobilize the NEA, the NASSP, and a host of other civil rights organizations and education associations to pressure President Nixon, the US Department of Justice (DOJ), the FBI, the US Department of Health, Education, and Welfare (HEW), and Congressional education committees in both houses to investigate and remedy the illegal and discriminatory treatment of Black principals.

THE NASSP TAKES A STAND

A Minnesota NASSP leader named David W. Meade was one convert in this crusade. Meade was so concerned that he wrote to his US Senator, Walter F. Mondale. His September 24, 1970, letter explained, "During this past weekend I attended a meeting in New Orleans which was hosted by our national association, in which we heard from many of our Black brothers in the South." Meade's concise, six-point list went on to summarize the catastrophic impact of desegregation on the Black educator workforce across the South:

1. The State of North Carolina has sent 195 Black senior high school principals "promoted," laterally or otherwise, out of the principalship. In five years' time, the number of Black principals in North Carolina has decreased from 200 to 5 as of the beginning of this school year.
2. 53 Black principals lost their jobs in Alabama this year. One Alabama city dismissed all six principals within the city.
3. Black principals are convinced that there is a deep-rooted plan set up to allow this to happen.
4. Black schools are being closed more often than White schools, even though the building might be better and both schools are needed in the community to contain the students.
5. In many cases, Black principals who are certificated and have years of service in the community are being replaced by White principals who have neither the certification nor the experience in either the position or the community.
6. Frequently, White principals are being put in charge of all Black schools after the Black principal has been dismissed.[2]

Meade explained that a month before the national school principals' 1970 annual meeting, NASSP President J. Frank Malone had requested that US Attorney General John N. Mitchell investigate the illegal and discriminatory treatment of Black principals. Malone's August 24 letter called for legal remedies and described the "extensive dimensions" of racially discriminatory dismissals, demotions and displacements of Black principals, "very much a reality . . . substantiated by many sources." [3]

To be sure, some of the NASSP's White members in the southern and border states were responsible for the mistreatment of Black principals and teachers. Until 1965, most border and southern states listed "White" and "colored" state chapters of the organization. Nonetheless, Malone told the attorney general that the NASSP was "deeply concerned with and perturbed by" the circumstances and "determined that it must be brought to an immediate and complete halt." Black principal dismissals and demotions represented a "discarding and waste of a significant and fine store of professional talent, training and experience," Malone wrote, and were a "blatantly illegal and immoral violation of . . . constitutionally guaranteed civil and economic rights." Malone asked for "the intervention of the federal government using its full force and power to bring it to an end."[4]

Malone also sent copies of his letter to President Nixon, HEW Secretary Elliot Richardson, Acting US Commissioner of Education Ted Bell, and the chairmen of the House and Senate Committees on Education. This forceful letter from one of the leading educational organizations in the US closed by calling on the attorney general to do the following:

1. To undertake an immediate and rapid investigation in every state as to the extent and degree to which desegregation of schools is resulting in the elimination and demotion of public-school administrators and supervisors based upon patterns of racial discrimination;
2. To issue due notice and warning to all school districts through the offices of the respective governors and chief state school officers that the federal government is determined to stop all such practices as illegally discriminatory acts in violation of the civil rights law of the United States;
3. To undertake appropriate legal steps to restrain and prosecute those responsible for such practices and to protect and give relief to the victims of such discrimination; and
4. To enlist the cooperation of all other appropriate federal departments and agencies such as the Department of Health, Education and Welfare and the United States Office of Education, as well as the federal courts, to effectuate immediate remedies to bring to an end such discriminatory practices within public school systems as well as giving direct personal assistance to those who have suffered from these practices.[5]

A week later, on August 31, 1970, the NASSP received a brief two-paragraph reply from Assistant Attorney General Jerris Leonard in response to Malone's eleven-paragraph petition. The organization was outraged.

According to Meade's letter to Senator Mondale, the assistant attorney general "said in effect that they would be happy to prosecute if we could come up with the evidence." Leonard's reply read, in part, "You will note that in the states covered by the Fifth Circuit (Alabama, Florida, Georgia, Louisiana, Mississippi, Texas,) not only are there non-discrimination requirements, but dismissed or demoted employees have the right to inspect the evaluation and criteria on which their dismissal or demotion was based. Many of the court orders also contain reporting provisions which furnish us information on which we may act. You can assist us in carrying out our responsibility by giving us the details of any complaints you receive."

Meade wanted Senator Mondale to intervene and assist with a strategy for proactive engagement by the DOJ. "Our feeling is that the investigative machinery is immediately available to the Attorney General's office, if he should care to investigate," Meade wrote, "and an investigation by his office would not leave the individuals involved as vulnerable to community pressures and reprisal as if we did the investigating." Subsequently, Mondale wrote the US Attorney General and asked to be kept informed about the legal steps the DOJ took to remedy the problem.[6]

By late October 1970, NASSP President Malone wrote the assistant attorney general again—this time expressing "serious dissatisfaction" with the earlier responses. Malone recounted that the attorney general's letter was the "subject of careful evaluation and study" by the organization's National Committee on the Status and Welfare of Secondary School Administrators. During the NASSP's annual conference, that committee met with state affiliate representatives from Alabama, Mississippi, Louisiana, North Carolina, Florida, and Virginia; the committee's consensus was that the DOJ's course of action was not only "too little and probably too late, but one that demonstrated a lack of serious concern with the problem." In the NASSP's view, the attorney general was placing an unusually heavy burden on those Black principals victimized by illegal conduct. Malone charged, "Your letter to us seems to place the entire onus of the struggle to end these dismissals and demotions upon those who have been victimized by the process. You indicate that employees who have been dismissed or demoted 'have the right to inspect the evaluation and criteria on which their dismissal or demotion was based.' There is small comfort in such a right because it can be exerted only after the fact."[7]

Like everyone else who looked, Malone recognized that Black principals were already working under extremely hostile circumstances. Those who chose to fight against illegal mistreatment also faced "burdens of proof, legal action, economic costs, anxiety, time and public identification as a 'trouble-maker.'" Meanwhile, White boards of education, superintendents, and principals who perpetrated illegal acts against Black educators were able to rely on public funds and resources "to defend their actions and to save them harmless," even if they were later proved to have acted wrongly.[8]

With little other choice before them, the NASSP's officers agreed to turn over every complaint received. As providence would have it, the NASSP was able to rely on the work of the NAACP and Black educator associations in Georgia, North Carolina, Mississippi, and Louisiana, all of which completed numerous county-by-county and state-by-state reports containing detailed accounts of the atrocities. Still, Malone described the attorney general's recommendation as "treatment of the symptoms rather than an attack on the focus of the infection" and saw "little really effective remedy in such a course of action" but for a few individuals who had "both the courage to complain and knowledge as to where to direct such complaints."

BLACK EDUCATORS' DEMAND: ENFORCE THE *SINGLETON* DECREE

Malone closed the NASSP's second letter to Assistant Attorney General Leonard with several recommendations. First, he took issue with Leonard's statement that the DOJ was actively seeking to uphold the protections already put in place through to a landmark 1969 decision known as the *Singleton* decree.

In the three years immediately after the landmark Civil Rights Act of 1964, *Singleton v. Jackson Municipal Separate School District I and II*, along with two other decisions (*United States v. Jefferson County Board of Education* and *Green v. County School Board*) transformed school desegregation law and provided needed ammunition in Black educators' fight against racial discrimination. These opinions, issued in sequential cases from 1965 to 1968, were "laced with phrases of urgency" and declared that "the time has come for foot-dragging public school boards to move with celerity toward desegregation."[9]

Articulated by Judge John Minor Wisdom, these bold judicial decisions pressed for a compensatory justice that proclaimed that school boards had "the affirmative duty to take whatever steps might be necessary to convert to a unitary system in which racial discrimination would be eliminated root and branch" and to discard a "piecemeal approach to school desegregation in favor of a comprehensive view, addressing student and faculty assignment, transportation, and curriculum."[10]

According to Judge Wisdom, school boards had an affirmative constitutional duty to integrate, not merely to stop segregating. *Brown*, therefore, was not just a dispute between "individual Negro children and the state"; to the contrary, Wisdom held that Blacks had been "collectively harmed when the state, by law or custom operate[d] segregated schools."[11] Without this distinction, *Brown* could only benefit those children whose parents had the resources and courage to litigate segregated schools.

Wisdom pressed the states to move beyond desegregation to integration. Granting individual Blacks an equal educational opportunity was not enough; rather, "the only adequate redress for a previously overt system-wide policy of segregation directed against Negroes as a collective entity is a system-wide policy of integration." With these decisions, an end to *Brown II*'s mere "deliberate speed" dawned. School boards were charged "to come forward with a plan that promises realistically to work, and promises realistically to work, *now*."[12]

The *Singleton* case figured prominently in the arguments for displaced Black educators, but ultimately, the decision proved an insufficient mandate. The court ruled in *Singleton* that during the desegregation process, teachers and school administrators had to be hired, assigned, promoted, paid, demoted, and dismissed without regard to race, color, or national origin. It also held that staff be assigned so that the ratio of Black to White staff in each school be substantially the same as staff ratios in the entire school system. If a reduction in the number of principals, teachers, and other professional staff in a school district was necessary, staff members were to be selected for removal on the basis of objective, nondiscriminatory criteria (made public and maintained by each school district) developed prior to staff reductions. *Singleton* mandated that a position vacancy could not be filled by a person of a race, color, or national origin different from that of the individual dismissed or demoted, until each displaced staff member who was qualified had an opportunity to fill the post and had turned it down.

Though subsequent court rulings forcefully reaffirmed *Singleton's* prescriptions, the decimation of the ranks of Black principals persisted. The problems were due in part to the "insufficiencies in *Singleton* itself" and the failure of the Nixon administration to "coordinate and effectuate the letter and spirit of *Singleton*." As Black principal displacement progressed, *Singleton* proved "inherently insufficient," because it "did not contain any specific safeguards against racially discriminatory hiring, recruiting or promotion—other than the general prohibition against racial discrimination." Even with the ruling, school districts had "sufficient latitude to discriminate" because the court had "left the method of conversion entirely to the same state and local authorities who had maintained the dual system for 15 years after *Brown*."[13]

The NASSP's Malone was blunt in his assessment of the government's adherence to *Singleton*: "Unhappily, we must come to the conclusion that while, on paper, the Department supports a policy with which we are in full accord," he wrote, "there is little evidence emerging from the excessive dismissals and demotions of Negro educators to show that the policy has been enforced very actively or extensively."[14]

With little hope that the Department of Justice would assert itself, the NASSP nonetheless urged three new actions, bolstered by the NEA in *amicus curiae* briefs filed in multiple states. First, the NASSP recommended that the DOJ immediately notify all governors and members of the Chief State School Officers and School Superintendents Association (now the Council of Chief State School Officers) about the parameters of *Singleton*, which required that any principal or teacher dismissed or demoted as part of an overall reduction in staff resulting from court-ordered conversion to a unitary school system must be selected on the basis of objective and reasonable nondiscriminatory standards. Second, it reiterated its demand that the DOJ undertake full and complete investigations of each prior case of school desegregation to determine compliance with *Singleton*, and in those events where noncompliance was found, to secure relief for those who had suffered. Third, it wanted the DOJ to require an official statement from all actively desegregating school districts indicating that they were meticulously following *Singleton*.

Like the NASSP, the National Education Association pressed for stricter enforcement of the rulings in the *Singleton* cases. In its *amicus curiae* brief, the NEA's attorneys maintained that "many school districts bound by *Singleton* . . . eliminated a large number of their Black teachers and principals and . . . raised significantly the district's ratio of White to Black educators."[15]

"*Singleton* is not enough" and it "is insufficient in four respects," the NEA argued.[16] In its appeal to the court to amend and enforce the decision, it made the following points:

1. In its dependence on case-by-case litigation to challenge the standards used by school systems in terminating or demoting faculty members pursuant to a reduction in force, it places too great a burden on Black educators;
2. It does not provide workable safeguards against racial discrimination in terminations and demotions made for reasons other than reductions in force;
3. It does not provide specific safeguards against racially discriminatory hiring and promotions; and
4. It does not require school districts actively to recruit Black teachers and administrators.[17]

Even with the order to base reductions in staff on objective, nondiscriminatory, and public criteria, *Singleton* was unable to "stem the tide of discriminatory reductions" of Black educators. According to the NEA, "the decline in Black teachers and principals between 1968 and 1970, while Whites were increasing, shows that school districts still have too much latitude. They can eliminate Black educators in gross when they are left to their own devices in fashioning what may or may not be objective criteria."[18]

Pointing to statistical data about the elimination of Black principals and the court's ruling that delays in faculty desegregation were no longer tolerable, the NEA declared that further remedial action was needed to "preserve the rights of school children to a desegregated education . . . protect Black educators from discriminatory personnel policies, and avoid annual litigation seeking to roll back the school boards yearly hiring and firing."[19]

Significantly, *Singleton* had not placed an affirmative duty on school boards to recruit Black educators. NEA believed that "such a duty should be levied against those school districts that have diminished the ratio of Black to White educators" to offset racial imbalances caused by discriminatory hiring and firing. The NEA predicted two outcomes of its recommendations. First, such action would "help overcome the chilling effect that racial discrimination" was having on Black educators. Second, it would "help compensate for the reductions in the ranks of the major recruiter of Black teachers—the Black principal."[20]

Prior to the *Singleton* decision, the groundbreaking Civil Rights Act of 1964 had issued a national call for an end to discrimination on the basis of race, color, sex, and national origin in federally assisted programs. Three provisions of the law were specifically related to school desegregation. First, Title VI provided federal agencies, including HEW, with the ability to withhold federal funds from any noncompliant program or activity. Second, it allowed the DOJ to initiate lawsuits against recalcitrant school districts. Third, it prohibited racial discrimination in any program or activity receiving federal funds.

Paradoxically, although the Civil Rights Act held the promise of coercing districts into eliminating staff segregation, Black principal and teacher displacement accelerated after it was passed. Now, under more forceful laws requiring them to desegregate, school districts in border and southern state responded by closing Black schools. Revisions to the act in 1966 "impose[d] a 'positive duty' on the part of school districts to make 'significant progress' in eliminating staff segregation."[21]

By 1968, tighter revisions to Title VI held that students were the intended beneficiaries of faculty desegregation, and therefore, school districts were required to eliminate segregated faculties. Under these revisions, school districts had a duty—for the first time—not just to desegregate, but to integrate school staff. Using the teeth of the revised act, the Secretary of HEW terminated federal funds to districts that operated schools "in a racially discriminatory manner contrary to the requirements of . . . the Civil Rights Act."[22] Between 1968 and 1970, nearly 120 school districts had federal funding pulled. According to the NEA, although these districts were surely undercounted due to "self-serving accounts" of what was happening, there were fifty-two such districts in 1968, sixty-seven in 1969, and forty-eight in 1970.

Yet despite Supreme Court decisions in *Brown I* and *II*, the constitutional guarantees of the Fourteenth Amendment, the Civil Rights Act, and numerous circuit court of appeals decisions, the decimation of the ranks of Black principals and teachers continued. Between 1965 and 1973, a series of other judicial decisions pushed local districts to eliminate all vestiges of segregated schools, including segregated administrative staff and faculty. Where dual systems of public education existed, the law "cast the burden onto the school board to prove that its hiring practices were not discriminatory."[23] Additionally, the court found that "school authorities have an affirmative duty to break up the historical pattern of segregated faculties, the hallmark of the dual system" [and that] "school authorities bear the burden of justifying an apparent lack of progress." Under these conditions, Black educators who had been deprived of their positions by local school authorities turned to the courts for redress. These principals and teachers were not content to accept the jobs beneath their professional training and experiences offered by local school boards and superintendents but sought full relief under state law and the Constitution. Many succeeded.

Litigated in 1971 under one of many iterations of *Lee v. Macon County Board of Education*, the case of Charles Carter stands out. In 1967, Carter lost his job as principal of the all-Black school in Muscle Shoals, Alabama, that he had led for eight years, after it was closed pursuant to a court desegregation order. He then sought a new appointment as principal of the desegregated school. Carter was six hours from earning a master's degree and held state certificates qualifying him to serve as an assistant superintendent, principal, guidance counselor, and a teacher of social studies, English, and physical education. Instead of being appointed principal, however, he was passed over three times and offered a position as a Head Start teacher, which he reluctantly accepted. Later, he left the Head Start program and continued applying for principalships in the district. Offered none, he became a physical education teacher in 1970 and a seventh-grade social studies teacher in 1971. Finally, Carter sued the school district, alleging that he was denied principal and assistant principal appointments because of his race. The alleged discriminatory treatment was in violation of the Fourteenth Amendment of the Constitution (equal protection under the law) and numerous court directives, particularly those in *Singleton* and in earlier versions of *Lee*. Specifically, *Lee* held that the school board was not "free to recruit a new man to fill such a position until it had first offered the job to those . . . principals being demoted. Such persons could be bypassed only if they were not 'qualified' for the position."

In the court's view, Carter was not only "eminently qualified for the principalship, but also comparatively more qualified than the White vice-principal who was hired over him."[24] In fact, professional academic qualifications were not the determining factor that explained why Carter had not been selected for a principalship or assistant principalship in Muscle Shoals School System.

When asked why Carter had been passed over in favor of a White applicant, the district superintendent responded, "We felt at the time it was in the best interest not only of the school, but in the best interest for Mr. Carter because of the small percentage ratio of negro [sic] students."

The Fifth Circuit of the US Court of Appeals awarded Carter back pay and retirement benefits dating back to the denial of the principal post he sought in 1971. He was also awarded the difference in pay between his salary as a physical education teacher and the salary he would have earned as principal. In reversing the lower court's decision and demanding "immediate reinstatement, back pay, back retirement benefits and such other relief" for Charles Carter, the court fumed at the Muscle Shoals school district officials for their illegal and discriminatory treatment of Black principals and teachers:

> It is regrettable that the nation's constitutional journey toward equal protection of the laws for all Americans in the area of education must often run a course through the private and professional lives of individual students, teachers, and administrators. The undisputed testimony in this record is that during a four-year period, Charles Carter was not offered a smidgeon of a position within the Muscle Shoals school system. He was relegated out of the school system in defiance of *Singleton's* teachings, and finally in violation of *Singleton's* letter. We realize that there are shoals to be crossed in the treatment of faculty while desegregation proceeds, but the Black teacher must not be the only one to be stranded while positions are filled by Whites from afar. Because Muscle Shoals failed to comply with the laws and the Constitution with regard to activities and employments closely associated with the desegregation of the educational processes, the case of Charles Carter is reversed in part and remanded for immediate reinstatement, back pay, back retirement benefits, and such other relief and proceeding as the district judge may require.[25]

Like Carter, Amos Malone filed suit against Colbert County, Alabama, in August 1973, also under the *Lee* decision. Malone was principal of the all-Black Barton-Red Rock Elementary School, which was closed by court order. As a result, Malone was removed from the principalship and offered a teaching post, although he was assured by the school board that he would be given due consideration for future principal vacancies for which he was qualified. Thereafter, elementary principal vacancies occurred, but Malone was not offered an appointment. The school board contended that Malone was not qualified and filled all vacancies with Whites. Malone filed suit in district court, which ruled in his favor. On appeal, the US Court of Appeals for the Fifth Circuit concurred with the district court judge, who had filed his order the year before (in July 1972) in favor of Malone, finding that given Malone's qualifications, he was entitled to appointment to one of the principalship vacancies.

In *McCurdy v. Board of Public Instruction of Palm Beach County*, the US Fifth Circuit Court of Appeals determined that the school board violated the Fourteenth Amendment rights of Charles M. McCurdy, the Black principal of a predominantly Black senior high school, by failing to appoint him principal of a newly integrated senior high school. The court found that the board's position that McCurdy was not qualified did not have ample factual support. The school district was ordered to appoint McCurdy principal of the integrated high school and pay back salary and retirement benefits covering the four years that had elapsed since his original application for the position.

As late as 1977, the US Circuit Court of Appeals for the Fourth Circuit ruled in favor of another Black principal, Cornell Reynolds. In this case, the court found that within a year after school desegregation in Abbeville County, South Carolina, the number of Black principals had decreased by 75 percent, while contemporaneously, the number of White principals increased 11 percent, reducing the overall percentage of Black principals in the school system from 31 percent to 9 percent. (Prior to desegregation, 32 percent of the district's teachers were Black, but one year later, 29 percent were Black and the percentage of White teachers remained stable.)

When Abbeville desegregated, two Black elementary schools were closed. Reynolds, the principal of one, was transferred to a newly created position as administrative assistant to the superintendent. The district's other Black principals were assigned to assistant principalships and later also as administrative assistants to the superintendent.

School authorities never introduced any evidence that Reynolds's performance as a principal or teacher was unsatisfactory. Nonetheless, district school authorities testified that he was never considered for a principalship of an integrated school even though he held bachelor's and master's degrees, had pursued postgraduate studies, earned an A on the National Teachers

Examination, and was clearly qualified to teach in both elementary and secondary schools.[26] According to case records, the district superintendent, Robert H. Gettys, said "he made a subjective judgment about the best person for the job; other qualities might be more important than level of certification, but he had not articulated objective standards to guide his selections." In fact, the court records explained that the superintendent testified that Reynolds was not even considered for a principal vacancy previously held by a White male. "Although Reynolds had been a principal and teacher for twenty-five years," the records state, "a White man from another school system, with three years' experience as a high school classroom teacher, was hired to fill the vacancy."[27]

Superintendent Gettys further testified that Reynolds and Moore were hired as his administrative assistants because "the Black community distrusted the administration" and therefore, the assistant's primary role would be "helping members of his race by gaining their confidence." Reynolds and Moore, in contrast, saw the position as a dead-end, lackey, and demeaning one (and in fact, the position was eliminated after two years). In their testimony before the court, Reynolds and Moore stated that, as principals, they had the authority to set policies, supervise teachers, and direct the operations of a school. But as administrative assistants to the superintendent, they had no staff, no control over policies, and few defined duties. Both men testified that the administrative assistant's position was less prestigious and involved less responsibility than that of the principal. Indeed, Reynolds indicated that he had to write his own job description. After enduring a period without any responsibilities, Reynolds' first assignment was to accompany the district's attendance teacher to the homes of Black students. His second assignment was to evaluate teachers whom the administration considered weak—all but two of whom were Black.

Although it was in the central office, the position constituted a demotion in Reynolds's and Moore's eyes. Moore ultimately retired from the district due to health reasons, testifying, "I tried to do it until my health wouldn't let me, and I quit. I just quit because I was out there on a limb."[28] The court agreed that Reynolds had established a *prima facie* case of racial discrimination and ordered Abbeville County School District to reinstate him, consider him for the next vacant principalship, and provide back pay and other expenses incurred because of his illegal demotion and discharge.

THE NAACP: FIGHTING FOR BLACK EDUCATORS, FUNDING LITIGATION

In these and hundreds of other cases, Black principals as plaintiffs cultivated relationships with Black attorneys through the NAACP Legal Defense and Educational Fund (LDF), the Urban League, and members of the lesser-known Lawyers' Constitutional Defense Committee (LCDC). Formed in 1964, LCDC was a coalition of chief legal officers at several New York-based human and civil rights organizations, including the Congress of Racial Equality (CORE), the American Civil Liberties Union (ACLU), and the American Jewish Congress (AJC). Over an eight-year period, these organizations volunteered legal help and marshaled some 650 lawyers to defend clients fighting Jim Crow laws, primarily in the deep South.

Though Department of Justice attorneys were dispatched to investigate complaints, Black educators often found that these lawyers, who did not live in the South, typically took conservative positions and agreed to settle cases against the wishes of the complainants. To the contrary, through LCDC's corps of mainly Black (and some Jewish) attorneys, Black principals had access to lawyers who resided in southern states and were familiar with local conditions. In particular, NAACP LDF lawyers were well known for developing new theories of litigation that gained credibility, even with hostile district court judges, by repeatedly getting unfavorable decisions reversed on appeal.

Protracted litigation exacted a heavy financial burden. As early as 1955, Black teachers and principals had predicted a need for legal assistance, pledging $16,950 a year to the NAACP Legal Defense and Education Fund through the National Conference of State Teachers Associations, made up of Black teachers and principals associations in Alabama, Arkansas, Florida, Georgia, Louisiana, Mississippi, North Carolina, South Carolina, Oklahoma, Tennessee, Texas, and Virginia. As state chapters of Black teacher associations merged with the formerly all-White National Education Association, Black national leadership at NEA swelled and affected the organization's advocacy agenda. In 1965, the NEA Representative Assembly established the Million Dollar Fund "to promote and protect the professional, civil, and human rights of educators through legal and other necessary assistance."[29] The NEA's DuShane Fund, founded to protect teachers' rights, also figured prominently in combating the job losses experienced by Black educators. At the time of his testimony at the Senate hearings on July

15, 1970, NEA President George D. Fisher stated that the DuShane Fund had 181 applications from Black principals and teachers "alleging violation of their professional rights for reasons of race."[30] By 1979, the DuShane Fund's expenditures had reached $2.6 million, as the NEA's sponsorship and support of litigation increased tremendously—from 1,743 cases to 15, 614—in the four years between 1975 and 1979.[31]

THE NIXON ADMINISTRATION'S PERNICIOUS RESPONSE

During the spring and summer of 1970, the NAACP, NASSP, and NEA continued to urge the Nixon administration to write a memorandum to school districts detailing what was required to comply with provisions in the Civil Rights Act of 1964, particularly the provisions related to faculty and administrative hiring, firing, and demotion and displacement. The organizations warned federal officials of an expected increase in discrimination against Black educators and consulted with the HEW and DOJ about the specific wording of the memorandum. On August 6, 1970, HEW Secretary Richardson and Civil Rights Director Pottinger promised a US Senate Committee that the memorandum would probably be issued "within ten to fifteen days."

Instead, on December 12, 1970, the US Office of Education announced a $3.2 million training program to "assist teachers and administrators displaced by the process of desegregation" and to "improve and enlarge the skills of those displaced personnel who wished to remain in the education profession" [or] "who desire to enter other fields." The program was not a new commitment of resources. Rather, $3 million of this funding was extracted from a $4.9 million teacher training program already developed as a response to accusations from HBCU presidents that the Nixon administration was unsupportive of their colleges/universities. The $3 million allocation was distributed as follows: $2 million toward training demoted educators; $1 million for graduate fellowships for demoted Black educators who wished to remain in education; and new funds of $200,000 under the Manpower Development and Training Act for Black educators desiring to leave the field of education.

By early June of 1972, William C. Young, deputy commissioner of the US Office of Education, announced that the program—designed to reach 1,500

Black principals and teachers—had reached only 176 educators and would terminate by the end of the month. By June 30, 1973, funding for Southern University's Training and Coordination Center, a key site for the implementation of the training program, had also been withdrawn.

Nixon's launch of this dubious training program stood in odd juxtaposition to his March 24, 1970, *Statement about Desegregation of Elementary and Secondary Schools*, in which he seemed to indicate that he understood that Black teachers were being unfairly subjected to discrimination. "If school administrators were truly colorblind and teacher assignments did not reflect the color of the teacher's skin," the 1970 statement read, "the law of averages would eventually dictate an approximate racial balance of teachers in each within a system."[32] Not surprisingly, given the evidence that Black educators were typically as well as or better qualified than their White peers, civil rights organizations and education associations viewed the training program approach as dismissive of federal court decisions, unsympathetic to the plight of Black principals and teachers, and supportive of the myth that Black educators were the inferior professionals in the troubled landscape of desegregation.

Even the *New York Times*, which had previously devoted scant attention to the decimation of black educators in the desegregating South, derided this unasked-for retraining program. In a front-page story in December 1970 headlined "Agency to Train Negro Teachers Ousted in South," the *Times* wrote of the Nixon administration's "failure to challenge the legality of demoting hundreds of Negro teachers in the South" and pointed out the oddity of the administration's announcement of a $3.2 million training program for displaced Black teachers at the same time the US Office of Education released a study stating that "discrimination rather than inadequate training is the primary problem facing Black teachers in the South." The article concluded by quoting Jack Greenberg, head of the LDF, who called the training program "outrageous." "They should be spending the money enforcing the law, not only accepting the Southern assertion that 'Black teachers are untrained,'" Greenberg said. "The Administration is trying to buy off Negro teachers with a one-year training program."

By 1972, the Nixon administration's Office of Education had set up a Program for Displaced Students and Educators. The program's express purpose was to provide guidance to legal and education agencies responsible for helping displaced Black educators and students to "relocate and start new careers." The guiding document (the Guide) published by the office listed the university, legal, and financial resources available to forced out-of-work Black educators.

In large measure, the assistance offered was in the form of stipends paying off Black educators to go into junior college posts, K–3 teaching positions, and federally funded programs in special education and reading (which were usually subject to phase-out when soft money stopped flowing).

The Guide is a depressing glimpse into the fate of the affected Black principals and teachers. After all their efforts to play by the segregationist rules as they earned their advanced degrees and certifications, taught in inadequately funded and equipped schools, and fought for equal educational opportunity, they were shuffled off to the final humiliation with the false lure of professional development seminars, graduate school stipends they did not need, and jobs beneath their rank and calling and for which they had no interest.

To its credit, the Guide contained a state-by-state roll call of alarming statistics about Black educator displacement, making it clear that Black teachers and principals were subject to illegal firings, demotions, and displacement—just as documented repeatedly in the 1970 Senate hearing transcripts. The Guide also indicted the use of the Educational Testing Service's National Teacher Examination (NTE) as "another device being used against Black teachers."[33] On the heels of desegregation, many dual-system states instituted the NTE with the explicit purpose of eliminating Black teachers from the workforce. In many cases the strategy failed, but time would show that the early efforts to use new ETS-produced certification tests would end up being a trial run for later decades, up until the present time. In Louisiana, Mississippi, and Florida, for example, tests were dropped when White teachers were failing them at rates higher then Blacks. According to the Guide, "Florida began requiring a certain score on the NTE in 1961 but revoked the requirement several years later because many Whites were scoring poorly. An NEA task force discovered at least two Louisiana districts had tried the test but abandoned it when Whites scored low."[34]

For all the supposed sympathy and support offered by the US Office of Education's Displacement Program, its result was, in fact, to facilitate the final, insulting, and bureaucratic boot out of the profession's door—the back door—for the Black educators it purported to serve.

NIXON'S SOUTHERN STRATEGY AND THE ELIMINATION OF BLACK EDUCATORS

Nixon's detractors and supporters alike understood his announcement that desegregation had been accomplished and his introduction of the Black educator training program as a final retreat by the federal government and part and parcel of his "southern strategy"—a political effort to retain the support of conservative southern Democrats by appealing to their discontent with federal desegregation policies and a liberal Supreme Court. Almost immediately, six civil rights organizations—the American Friends Service Committee, the LDF, the Lawyers' Committee for Civil Rights Under Law, the Lawyers Constitutional Defense Committee, the Washington Research Project, and the Delta Ministry of the National Council of Churches—issued a report challenging the Nixon administration's assertion that desegregation had been accomplished. The group's report on the status of desegregation in the South (published by the American Friends Service Committee) called the training plan "an unfortunate program" [that] "accepts White southern school officials' belief that Black teachers and principals were qualified to teach Black children but not White children."[35] Supported by data gathered by monitors sent to more than four hundred school districts, the study provided an in-depth analysis of the plight of Black educators.

Chapter 3 of the report, titled "Racial Discrimination Against Black Teachers and Administrators," opened as follows: "That desegregation of a dual school system requires nondiscriminatory treatment and assignment of Black teachers, administrators, and other staff is now patently clear. Yet our monitors found widespread discriminatory dismissal and demotion of Black principals and teachers, and violations of legal requirements for racial assignment of staff."[36]

Three of the study's six recommendations referenced principal and teacher assignments:

- Black teachers, principals, coaches and other staff have been dismissed or demoted from their former positions in massive numbers throughout the "desegregated" South. Apart from the obvious humiliation and economic distress to these Black adults, this process is leading toward an all-White structure of authority in southern public schools.
- The assignment of faculty and staff has often been carried out so as to leave schools identifiable as Black or White, in clear violation of prevailing legal standards and HEW guidelines.

- The Departments of HEW and Justice have accepted some desegregation plans which will result in resegregation and which unnecessarily permit continuation of segregated schools.[37]

"Underlying these problems is the mistaken belief that desegregation is simply the mixing of Black and White students," the report asserted. These problems "could have been avoided by firm federal enforcement of existing legal standards," but the Nixon administration "consistently underdefined the legal requirements of school desegregation."[38] In fact, scolded the civil rights organizations, the administration had accepted weak desegregation plans, given reprieves to school systems that refused to meet Title VI compliance deadlines, and influenced federal courts to adopt plans that did not require desegregation of faculty and staff—all in direct violation of the law. Rather than attack segregated school districts by using the full investigatory and compliance machinery available, HEW changed the method of reporting public school desegregation from individual schools to districts. This methodology enabled the administration to compute statistics showing that all but 76 of 2,700 southern school districts were desegregated, that 90.5 percent of Black and White students were attending schools in a unitary system, and that unprecedented progress had been achieved in dismantling the dual system.

The problems of incomplete desegregation had to be dealt with, and civil rights organizations believed that the federal government had the power and resources to complete the job. To strengthen the federal response, the American Friends Service Committee report recommended that

1. The federal government secure through the courts and Title VI machinery desegregation plans which produce school systems without Black schools or White schools, but just schools;
2. In formulating desegregation plans, the federal government ensure that the burdens of desegregation be borne by Black and White equally, and that physically sound Black school buildings be used rather than closed;
3. The federal government mount a major national enforcement effort against in-school segregation and other forms of discrimination against Black children in public schools, using both the courts and the sanction of federal fund cutoffs provided by Title VI of the Civil Rights Act of 1964—in particular, that the Department of HEW

publish and enforce the memorandum prohibiting particular discriminatory practices against students which it prepared and promised to release last summer; and

4. The federal government enforce, through the courts and through Title VI fund cutoffs, existing legal standards prohibiting discrimination in the hiring, firing, promotion or demotion of Black principals, teachers and other school staff. In particular, that the Department of HEW release and enforce the memorandum prohibiting particular discriminatory practices against teachers which it prepared and promised to release last summer.[39]

Despite these recommendations and all the known transgressions against Black educators, defiance to desegregate with "all deliberate speed" simply increased the assault on Black principals and teachers.

BLACK AND WHITE: VIEWS FROM THE NEWS MEDIA

From 1970 until well into 1972, the national press, both Black and White, railed against the Nixon administration's response to the inequities of school integration. Though desegregation was a national issue warranting national coverage, elimination of Black educational leadership was largely confined to the southern states; media coverage did not assign this issue the same urgency in the national dialogue as it was experienced in the Black community. Yet Black educators' displacement, an issue of critical and lasting importance to the Black community, would eventually prove to be so to the rest of the nation as well.

Historically, the Black press was conceived as a partner in the struggle for human and civil rights. Begun in 1867 with the *Freedom's Journal*, Black newspapers were crafted as champions of equal rights for Blacks, advocating an end to discrimination in employment, education, and voting privileges. Through their opinion pieces and news analyses, these publications brought a perspective to issues often elided in the mainstream press, calling attention to race prejudice worldwide. Thus, it is no surprise that even into the 1970s, Black media coverage of Black educators' displacement exceeded that of the White media in scope, content, and frequency. Between 1970 and 1972, Black newspapers and periodicals such as the monthly *Ebony*, NAACP's *The Crisis*, and the weekly news magazine *Jet* published more than one hundred articles about Black principal and teacher displacement alone (in addition to other coverage about desegregation). These publications offered extensive interviews with leading government and education officials and affected educators. Some of this coverage was referenced in the 1971 Senate hearings about the displacement and status of Black principals.

For example, on the day of Nixon's retraining plan announcement, a *Washington Afro-American* headline proclaimed, "Teacher Firing Seen Promoted by Nixon Plan." Describing the plan as "perpetuating . . . discrimination through a program to retrain Black educators," E. B. Palmer, associate executive secretary of the North Carolina Teachers Association, was quoted as saying the plan was insulting and that Black educators resented it. "The very fact that this offer is being made to Black educators with no reference to preventive action against this practice of unfair, unethical, and discriminatory dismissal of Black educators, in itself supports and perpetuates the dismissal of Blacks," Palmer said. "No evidence has been produced which lays the basis for the conclusion that Black educators are incompetent and therefore need retraining."[40]

An April 1971 editorial column headline from the *Roanoke Tribune* in Virginia blasted "Virginia's Black Senior High School Principals Victims of Insidious Desegregation Blight"—and provided statistics about the damage being done.[41] Headlines from other Black newspapers throughout border and southern states revealed the tenor of coverage. These newspapers and others served as the "dominant means of communication of Black culture [and] functioned as the conduit through which Black news moved at a time when White Americans virtually ignored everything of real concern to Blacks."[42] All across the nation, "Blacks' problems and interests were remarkably similar" and Black newspapers like the *Afro-American*, *Chicago Defender*, and *Pittsburg Courier* carried extensive news and reports, and "hammered for equality" and integration.[43]

The Black press coverage of Black educators' plight was far more detailed and pervasive than the White press's attention. In many cases, Black newspaper articles read more like field research. Table 4.1 summarizes some of this coverage—all of which is included in the 1971 Senate Hearings on the Displacement of Black Principals.

As early as 1952, the popular and widely disseminated magazine *Jet Magazine: The Weekly Negro News Magazine* (created and produced by Black publisher John H. Johnson) ran an article about the disparity between Black

TABLE 4.1 Selected list of Black newspaper coverage of Black educator displacement

NAME OF NEWSPAPER AND YEAR FOUNDED	ARTICLE TITLE AND DATE	ABSTRACT
The Baltimore Afro-American *The Washington Afro American* (1892)	"School Mixing Is Accompanied by Discrimination," November 21, 1970	School desegregation in Louisiana and Mississippi has produced near-total disintegration of Black authority in every area of public education.
Atlanta Daily World (1928)	"Education Leaders Seek to Halt Teacher, Student Woes," February 14, 1973	Leaders of state education associations across the South have moved to curb the critical teacher and pupil displacement problem in the region.
Atlanta Daily World (1928)	"GTEA Asks HEW to Halt Mistreatment of Negroes," February 26, 1970	Dr. Horace E. Tate, executive secretary of the Georgia Teachers and Education Association, has been in Washington conferring with officials in the office of the US Commissioner of Education.
Atlanta Daily World (1928)	"Dr. Mays Speaks at Professor's Confab," August 27, 1971	Dr. Benjamin E. Mays says nobody knows how many Black teachers or principals have been demoted or have lost their jobs in the name of integration.
Chicago Defender (1905)	"NEA Finds 1,000 Black Educators Dropped in 3 Years," April 10, 1971	NEA proposes legal machinery aimed at eliminating the spread of racial discrimination against Black southern school faculties in wake of a disclosure that five thousand lost jobs.
Chicago Defender (1905)	"31,5000 Teachers Lose Jobs," June 5, 1973	Some 31,500 Black teachers have lost their jobs as a result of school integration in seventeen Southern states.
Chicago Defender (1905)	"The Trauma of Desegregating Schools," September 12, 1970	The Southern Regional Council reports experiences of Black students in desegregated schools and the rapidity with which private schools are springing up in many sections of the South.
New York Amsterdam News (1909)	"Integration—American Style," February 6, 1971	Integration "American style" is displacing more Black professionals than segregation ever did, especially in the field of education.
Wichita Times (1970)	"Desegregation Costing Blacks Jobs, Money, Education," June 14, 1973	Southern Black communities are thirty thousand jobs and $250 million poorer as a result of desegregation in the public schools, according to several educational and civil rights groups.

NAME OF NEWSPAPER AND YEAR FOUNDED	ARTICLE TITLE AND DATE	ABSTRACT
Milwaukee Star (1961)	"To Be Equal: The South's Purge of Black Teachers," June 21, 1973	Many Black teachers and administrators shunted off regular payrolls of school districts are placed in special compensatory education programs funded by the federal government.
Milwaukee Star (1961)	"School Desegregation Has Produced Discrimination, NEA Asserts," November 24, 1973	In St. James Parish, Louisiana, a Black principal with twenty-five years' experience and a master's degree has been demoted to "assistant visiting teacher."
Los Angeles Tribune (1945)	"Political What Not, No Negro Supervisors, Negro Senior High Principals," April 8, 1960	Negroes are complaining that there is a "limited ceiling" for Negro educators in supervisory or administrative positions in school district.
Newark Evening Star (1907)	"To Help Integration—Ousted Black Teachers and Principals," December 12, 1970	The Nixon administration releases funds to train 1,500 fired or demoted Black teachers and principals in the South because of desegregation.
The Roanoke Tribune (1939)	"Virginia Black Senior High School Principals Victims of Insidious Desegregation Blight," April 15, 1971	Black principals have been demoted and Black teachers replaced by the hundreds across the South.
Washington Afro-American (1892)	"Teacher Firing Seen Promoted by Nixon Plan," December 30, 1970	The Nixon administration perpetuates discrimination against Black educators.

and White educators' credentials titled "Alabama Black Teachers Hold More Degrees Than White Counterparts," highlighting the announcement made by Montgomery County's (Alabama) superintendent, Dr. Clarence M. Dannelly.[44] Between 1970 and 1972, *Jet*, more than any other publication, ran the most comprehensive series of articles about Black educator displacement. Though many article titles referenced teachers, significant attention was also devoted to the plight of principals. Its July 9, 1970, article, "Bias Against School Principals," began, "Even though Maryland Black educators are more highly educated than their White counterparts, only a handful are promoted to the post of principal, according to a [Maryland] State Board of Education report."[45] "Nixon's Plan to Retrain Fired Teachers Called Outrage," was the next headline in the series. This article quoted Jack Greenberg, head lawyer for the Legal Defense and Education Fund, Inc., who flared, "I think it is an outrage. They (the administration) ought to spend their resources to keep Black teachers [and principals] from being fired instead of giving this bribe to keep quiet." NEA President Helen Bain weighed in as equally critical of the Nixon administration's response to Black educators' plight. "We seriously question whether any so-called retraining proposal, however well-motivated, is meaningful in light of the federal government's failure to challenge the legalities of wholesale firing and demotion of Negro teachers [and principals] in the South," Bain said.[46]

In its next article, "Government Ponders Plan to Help Black Teachers in Desegregated Schools," the magazine cited a study by Samuel B. Ethridge, the NEA's assistant executive secretary for teachers' rights. The study found that six thousand Black principals had lost their jobs since 1954. Ethridge charged that President Nixon's response did not address the real cause of displacement in desegregated schools—racism. "As far as handling the causes of displacement, this plan is not the answer," Ethridge said. "We have documented cases where Black teachers with doctoral and master's degrees have been displaced or put into subordinate positions. These people do not need additional training. They were dismissed because they are Black."[47]

In the same *Jet* issue, William C. Young, deputy commissioner of the Office of Education, described specific provisions of the Nixon retraining program. According to Young, the program provided legal fees for seventy-five displaced Black educators, a maximum of $1,000 for six hundred unemployed educators to move their families to new locations, and 528 stipends at $6,600 each for college tuition and living expenses of Black educators who desired further training.

Interestingly, *Jet* and the national weekly *Time* each covered the case of the same displaced Black principal, a Louisiana educator named Fred McCoy. *Jet* provided a thorough profile of McCoy as a thirty-nine-year-old father of two children and a nine-year veteran in the education profession, printing an interview with him that included his jarring reaction to the Nixon administration's training program:

> [McCoy] calmly explained his predicament: "I was demoted from principal to a 4th-grade classroom teacher under a White principal who required that I put out chairs in the auditorium, put chalk in each classroom, toilet tissue in the boys' bathroom, and pick up paper from the lawn." . . . After

[the all-Black school] was closed he was assigned to Natalbany Elementary School [formerly all-White] as a part-time janitor and then transferred to teach math to 4th to 6th grade. His salary was cut $3,226.84. To make up for the losses McCoy worked evenings at the Edward Hines Sawmill in Fluker, Louisiana, for $1.60/hour (minimum wage). The father of two children told *Jet*, "It has been rather degrading for a principal to work (at a sawmill) with students I have taught and informed to stay in school so that they may get an education and make a decent living."

> Nothing has been done at the federal level and US Attorney John N. Mitchell was accused of showing "blatant disregard of the rights of Black teachers in the South" and moral treason for not investigating NEA reports of discrimination in desegregating districts by James H. Williams, director of NEA's southeast regional office.[48]

By comparison, on July 13, 1970, *Time* magazine (largely oriented to White audiences) devoted much less attention to McCoy's "appalling case." In "The Bad Side of Integration," *Time* reported, "Integration closed his [McCoy's] school, and he was assigned to teach a fourth-grade class at a formerly all-White school—in the morning. In the afternoon, he was expected to do janitor's chores in the school latrines. At least McCoy kept busy. A Black former principal in Louisiana has been given a desk to sit at but no title or duties."[49]

Jet also covered the oddest plan to eliminate Black school leaders—one unreported in any other news outlet. A headline on May 16, 1971, described a "scurrilous campaign" to rid the state of Black principals: "Mississippi White Women Offered $500 Reward to Use Sex as Trap to Rip Off Black Males." The *Jet* reporter interviewed Mississippi NAACP and other community leaders and quoted civil rights activist Fannie Lou Hamer about the "anti-Black school official project," which Hamer said required White female (and male) agents to accuse Black male (and female) principals and teachers of fake sexual crimes with White victims. A Mississippi state field director for the NAACP reported that the plan was responsible for the dismissal of at least one Black male principal:

> Five hundred dollars will be awarded to any White woman responsible for the permanent elimination of Black males from our public schools," the mimeographed leaflet began. . . . "Maneuver a Black man into a

> compromising position. Arrange with a friend to witness the affair. Be sure that there are no other witnesses. Once you have them in the position, protest and run."
>
> Though not mentioned prominently in the leaflet, Black women were also cited as targets. In a final note, the leaflet said, "Remember our boys can also follow this procedure to eliminate Black female teachers and principals . . . When the Black that you have accused is permanently discharged . . . we will forward your check. Our organization is dedicated to the permanent elimination of Blacks from high positions in our public schools . . . and the return of public schools to Whites."
>
> Civil rights activist Fannie Lou Hamer weighed in on whether the "anti-Black school official leadership project" was a hoax. Hamer said, "It's probably no hoax. You don't know these fools like we know them down here."[50]

Jet's analysis of the illegal efforts to dismantle Black school leadership continued in a series of five articles well into the late 1970s. The first article in the series, titled "The Crisis," signaled the gravity of the concern to the Black community. The article reported a massive boycott of Memphis City Schools by Black educators and students and quoted the Memphis Board of Education's response to an NAACP complaint that it "did not intend to work toward racial balance at the administrative level."[51] According to a September 1971 article, the NAACP complained to HEW Secretary Richardson that the Bullock County (Alabama) Board of Education was continuing to employ a disproportionate number of White principals, teachers, and teachers' aides—and fire Blacks in those roles—even though the district's student population of slightly over 1,300 students was 99 percent Black. The article reported that the NAACP was successful in its effort to have federal funding revoked from the district.[52]

Ebony magazine, another prominent publication founded by Johnson—begun in 1945 and the nation's first Black-oriented magazine to attain national circulation—also ran lengthy analyses about the decimation of Black teachers and principals in a series of three articles. An article in the August 1971 issue, "The Dixie School Charade: Blacks are Deceived by Desegregation Pretense," presented the LDF's perspective about the Nixon plan. "The NAACP Legal Defense Fund criticized a recent Government proposal to make available $3.2 million to retrain Black teachers in the South," *Ebony*'s reporter explains. "LDF suggests that rather than accept at face value statements that Black teachers and principals are untrained, the Government should use the money to enforce the law. Currently representing dismissed Black educators in 35 court cases, LDF has established the legal principle that if an all-Black school is phased out, its Black staff cannot simply be fired."[53]

The article also presented research from the Atlanta-based Southern Regional Council and the NEA and discussed the deleterious effect the loss of Black educators was having on Black students: "Compounding the hurt, Black students find that the authority figures who once gave them pride and a sense of security—generally their Black principals, but also many of their Black teachers and coaches—have been demoted, dismissed outright, denied new contracts or pressured into resigning, and the less educated, less experienced teachers hired to replace them include fewer Blacks."[54]

Ebony's January 1972 issue featured an annual progress report for the nation's Black population in nine areas: education, government, business, employment, armed forces, arts and letters, religion, sports, and entertainment. The education section concluded, "Black educators, particularly principals, have borne the burdens incident to desegregation measures greatly disproportionate to any burdens borne by White educators."[55] Finally, the magazine's entire May 1974 issue was devoted to "The South Today" and contained a lengthy article, "Whatever Happened to School Desegregation?" referencing NEA's research that Black educator displacement resulted in a $240.5 million loss to the Black community. The article provided a status update about districts under court order and linked tensions in desegregated schools to several causes: "School confrontations have been provoked through discriminatory disciplining of Black students, through malicious display of Confederate symbols, and through the massive displacement of Black principals." The article concluded, "Allegedly desegregated schools still operate on terms set by Whites, governed by White rules and committed to perpetuating White values, attributes and traditions."[56]

By April 1973, *Ebony* and *Jet* reflected the Black community's strategy to acquire superintendencies and board of education posts, both of which were elected rather than appointed positions in many border and southern states. *The Crisis*'s "Why Black Candidates Lose in Mississippi" examined the compromising choreography between economic and political independence forced on southern Blacks as they sought control of desegregating public schools. The article asserted that "Whites consciously violate the law" in order to maintain power, and "the White power structure encourages Blacks to 'sell out' because it keeps a lid on the few jobs that exist."[57] As *The Crisis* reported: "Mrs. Eva Sherrod, a Black woman, announced she was going to run for county superintendent of education. But she didn't. A. R. Koon, the White superintendent who was a candidate for re-election and under whom Mrs. Sherrod had once worked, rehired and promoted her in the school system. Once an active participant in Black community affairs, she became an active non-participant."[58]

Sherrod's initial goal to become a superintendent reflected a long-held goal of Black principals, teachers, and other citizens. Though she was coerced into acceptance of the old and continuing order, the cause was not lost. Others would remain true to task. By the early 1970s, Black educators' desire to attain school districts superintendencies resulted in a strategy to do so: the establishment and launch of the National Alliance of Black School Educators (NABSE) in 1973 by Dr. Charles Moody. Like other founding NABSE members, Dr. Moody had attended an HBCU, earned his doctoral degrees at a top-tier predominantly White institution, and served as a public school teacher and administrator in segregated and desegregated schools. The NABSE, established to further academic achievement of all students—in particular, Black students—began as a preeminent collective of Black superintendents, central office directors, principals, and teachers with an annual conference designed for professional networking, sharing research, and developing education policies that would advance their mission to ensure that Black students in desegregated schools were getting a fair chance to succeed.

DESEGREGATION AND RACIAL UPLIFT: THE LINKS, BOULÉ, AND THE DIVINE 9

Black churches are usually mentioned as organizing forces in the fight for desegregation and civil rights, and deservedly so. However, there were (and are) many Black civic and social organizations, including Black sororities and fraternities, that have long been committed to assertively advancing desegregation and fighting for Black educators. Operating within a broader American society of "narrowly circumscribed opportunity and no security," Black civic and social organizations brought "social purpose and social action" to Black communities at the local level.[59]

Unlike churches, these civic, social and fraternal organizations had an infrastructure that spanned national, regional, and local offices, chapters, and membership. This infrastructure ensured that these organizations would be long-lasting and impactful.[60] They included The Links (founded in 1946), Sigma Pi Phi Fraternity (founded in 1904 and best known as "the Boulé"), and the Divine 9 (collectively, nine historically Black Greek letter organizations [i.e., sororities and fraternities]). The Divine 9, all of which still exist today, include:

- Alpha Phi Alpha Fraternity, founded 1906, Cornell University
- Alpha Kappa Alpha Sorority, founded 1908, Howard University
- Kappa Alpha Psi Fraternity, founded 1911, Indiana University
- Omega Psi Phi Fraternity, founded 1911, Howard University
- Delta Sigma Theta Sorority, founded 1913, Howard University
- Phi Beta Sigma Fraternity, founded 1914, Howard University
- Zeta Phi Beta Sorority, founded 1920, Howard University
- Sigma Gamma Rho Sorority, founded 1922, Butler University
- Iota Phi Theta Fraternity, founded 1963, Morgan State University

Historically, members of The Links, Boulé, and Divine 9 were viewed as the educated and social elite. In some ways, they established "an aristocracy—such as never existed before and perhaps never will exist again in America—midway between the white and black world."[61] However, this "aristocracy" was just as susceptible to the "virus of race madness" and could have their lives snuffed out and ambitions foiled by it, just as much as other Blacks.[62] Black fraternities and sororities worked through their membership to support civil rights organizations financially and to lobby for "social betterment and social action":[63]

> For decades, black fraternal networks had been helping to lay the groundwork for the major civil rights campaigns that culminated in the Civil Rights Act of 1964. In 1938 Alpha Kappa Alpha Sorority, Incorporated, created the National Non-Partisan Lobby on Civil and Democratic Rights (NPC), later renamed the National Non-Partisan Council on Public Affairs. It was the first full-time congressional lobby for minority group civil rights. Throughout the organization's life, the NPC worked with a range of other organizations that sought similar ends. The NPC was dissolved in

> 1948. In place of the NPC, Alpha Kappa Alpha established the American Council on Human Rights (ACHR) with the help of Delta Sigma Theta, Zeta Phi Beta, and Sigma Gamma Rho sororities as well as Alpha Phi Alpha, Phi Beta Sigma, and Kappa Alpha Psi fraternities.[64]

By necessity, the mission of The Links, Boulé, and the Divine 9 extended beyond social activities. Though not sufficiently acknowledged for such, these organizations and their members had (and continue to build) distinguished histories of public service tied to racial uplift and equality. Nonetheless, the noted sociologist E. Franklin Frazier, himself a member of Alpha Phi Alpha fraternity, criticized Black fraternities and sororities as "more concerned with consumption than racial activism."[65] Yet many members viewed themselves as bearing responsibility to help improve conditions for Black people, the nation, and the world—beliefs reflected in their personal and professional lives and their organizations' missions, work, and priorities. Many were public school teachers and university faculty members, among other professions (physicians, dentists, attorneys, nurses, and social workers). More often than not, they were also married and raising children. All of these circumstances conspired to fuel concern about the status of public schools for their children, as well as concerns about the education professions. Each of the women's groups, in particular, advanced national initiatives and programs that advocated for Black principal and teacher salary equalization and the Fair Employment Movement to eliminate employment discrimination based on race.

One of the Delta Sigma Theta's founders, teacher Jessie McGuire Dent, and her chapter were one example of such activism. When she learned that the state set Black teachers' and principals' salaries at 20 percent less than those for White principals and teachers, Dent sued the Galveston (Texas) Independent School District. Deltas in the Galveston community mobilized to help Dent's case, and she won a landmark victory in 1953 that gained equal pay for Black teachers in the district. The economic impact of Dent's legal victory would be felt for years to come.

Nationwide, Delta Sigma Theta members were also instrumental in writing reports and sharing information about the impact of the *Brown* decision on Black educators' job security. Though Black educators had worked with the NAACP to provide information that led to the historic *Brown* decision, when it came down from the Supreme Court, many Black educators worried about how White superintendents would respond to the decree and what this would mean for their jobs. Delta Sigma Theta members' reports and information sharing helped to quell anxiety in Black communities and informed the NAACP's ongoing strategy to protect Black educators' job and morale.[66]

The Links and Black sororities financially supported the NAACP, the Congress on Racial Equality (CORE), and the Committee for a Representative School Board and helped establish the American Council on Human Rights. Members also established Black newspapers to help mobilize the community and spread the word about problems and strategies for progress. Many successful voting rights and literacy campaigns were organized by these women in the early- and mid-1900s, often at great risk to their personal and family safety. Having the ability to vote was viewed by these women as a local imperative providing Black citizens a say in local elections of school boards and superintendents (many of which were elected, not appointed positions).

Black fraternities also stood up. A large number of men in these organizations were attorneys, physicians and dentists, university presidents, professors, and public school principals. Remarkably, many were lead attorneys litigating *Brown*, Black principal and teacher salary equalization cases, and employment discrimination lawsuits. In fact, both Charles Hamilton Houston (the first Black person to earn a doctorate at Harvard) and his mentee, Thurgood Marshall (who litigated and won *Brown* and became the nation's first Supreme Court Justice who was Black), were members of Alpha Phi Alpha. Omega Psi Phi members James Madison Nabrit Jr., Oliver Hill, and William Henry Hastie also litigated *Brown* and a number of foundational cases preceding it. Leon A. Ransom, a member of Kappa Alpha Psi, litigated groundbreaking Black teacher pay inequity lawsuits.

Ransom and other NAACP attorneys were successful in myriad cases. For more than twenty years prior to *Brown*, attorneys for the NAACP had partnered with Black principals and teachers in numerous lawsuits fighting pay inequities. The dual-system states were consistent—they enforced dual salary schedules that discriminated against Black educators, paying Blacks lower salaries even when they held educational qualifications, certifications, and other credentials equal to or superior to White educators. The Norfolk, Virginia, Public Schools salary schedule, for example, made the racial discrimination plain for all to see. (See table 4.2.) This state-sanctioned policy

TABLE 4.2 Negro and White teacher salaries in Norfolk, Virginia, 1940

	SALARIES NOW BEING PAID TEACHERS NEW TO THE SYSTEM	MAXIMUM SALARY BEING PAID (AFFECTING ONLY THOSE IN SYSTEM BEFORE INCREMENT PLAN WAS DISCONTINUED)
Negro		
Elementary		
• Normal certificate	$597.50	$960.10
• Degree	$611.00	$960.00
High school		
• Women	$699.00	$1,105.20
• Men	$784.50	$1,235.00
White		
Elementary		
• Normal certificate	$850.00	$1,425.00
• Degree	$937.00	$1,425.00
High school		
• Women	$970.00	$1,900.00
• Men	$1,200.00	$2,185.00

Source: Alston v. School Board of City of Norfolk, 112 F.2d 992 (4th Cir. 1940).

of differential pay based solely on race and color was unconstitutional and a violation of the Equal Protection Clause. Ransom's successful lawsuit against the City of Norfolk not only illuminated data about Black educators' credentials; it laid the foundation for future employment discrimination cases filed by displaced Black educators.

White media coverage of the illegal demotion and dismissal of Black principals and teachers was minimal. Only two *Washington Post* articles are cited in the Senate hearings, and those were published after a *Newark Evening News* article that was also appended to the hearings. A well-regarded daily, the *Newark Evening News* was heralded as the newspaper of record in New Jersey. It was the first in the White press corps to respond to Nixon's training proposal. Its December 12, 1970, article, "Nixon to Help Integration-Ousted Black Teachers, Principals," was critical of the administration's efforts and concluded with a quote from NEA's president: "Mrs. Helen Bain, president of the National Education Association, questioned the value of the training program and said she thought that the Black teachers were being displaced because of racial prejudice. 'If they need retraining now, they needed it years ago when they were teaching in Black schools,' she said in an interview. 'The real cause of this is the prejudice behind the thing.'"[67]

On February 27, 1971, the *Washington Post* devoted a brief thirteen lines to a DOJ lawsuit against a Mississippi schools district, concluding, "The government charged that prior to the opening of schools last fall [September 1970], the board discriminatorily fired at least 19 Black teachers and demoted 3 of the 4 Negro principals and all of the Black assistant principals in the school system."[68] On May 15, 1971, the *Post* ran a much lengthier article, "New Bias Problems Arise in South's Integrated Schools," that characterized the Nixon administration's response to the concern as reticent and piecemeal:

> This year . . . a new problem has grown up in the South: protecting the rights of those Black students and teachers once inside the buildings. The government has not yet decided whether or how to do it . . . Pottinger [director of HEW's Office of Civil Rights] himself acknowledges that, since they "moved the bodies" in September, HEW and the Justice Department have done relatively little in the South this school year, even on the issue of faculty integration spelled out in the January memo.[69]

The four-page article, however, devoted only a paragraph to the subheading "Blacks Demoted":

> Black principals have been demoted and Black teachers replaced with Whites by the hundreds across the South. The government itself, in one computer run last winter, found 1,666 Southern school districts in which the number of Black teachers fell by 30 percent—a total of 1,674—between 1968 and 1970. The number of White teachers rose by 1,491 in the same period. The flow of protest is another reflection of the racial rearrangement in the South.[70]

Of any White press, *The New Republic* magazine provided the most extensive examination of Black principal displacement. Its September 26, 1970, article, "Another Vanishing American: The Black Principal?" was authored by Dr. J. C. James, a Federal Executive Fellow of the Brookings Institution who had once served as associate dean of admissions at Howard University and chief of the Southern Branch of the Division of Equal Educational Opportunities in the Office of Education. Dr. James's article, essentially a treatise about the importance of the Black principal, reached an eloquently stated but startling conclusion. "Perhaps not since the Civil War has anything struck the South where it lives in the way that school desegregation has," Dr. James wrote. "For those caught in the vise created by the transition from dual to unitary school systems, the experience can be a disaster of major proportions for which there is no adequate recompense. The Black principal is a prime victim of this disaster."[71]

TOO LITTLE AND TOO LATE, INDEED

On August 6, 1970, HEW Secretary Richardson and Civil Rights Director Pottinger had promised to release a policy statement on faculty and staff desegregation. The memorandum, however, was not issued until almost a year later, on July 14, 1971. The missive affirmed the DOJ's adoption of *Singleton* as its official policy, promised to investigate those districts where Black principals and teachers had been substantially reduced, and required that educator recruitment be nondiscriminatory. However, the statement did not amend Nixon's December 1970 announcement, nor did it establish new protective measures for displaced Black educators. The administration continued its case-by-case approach, which meant a waiting period while aggrieved parties came forward with individual complaints. Many disagreed with this process and continued to urge the administration to use its "vast investigatory and prosecutorial machinery in an affirmative, energetic effort to find and extirpate discrimination."[72] Without an affirmative effort, results were "intolerably slow" and "piecemeal," and ultimately severely hurt Black principals and teachers. "Paradoxically, school desegregation . . . has victimized Black educators," William Jefferson wrote in the *Tulane Law Review*. "Preventive measures against displacement are nonexistent and after-the-fact remedies have proved inadequate. Even where favorable decrees are obtained, they often come too late to be truly remedial for the teacher [and principal] who has suffered displacement."[73]

Led by its Black Principals Caucus, the NASSP continued its assault on the issue of Black principal displacement. By November 1970, the organization's directors came together at the NASSP annual meeting and took a vote to "bring this increasingly serious problem to the direct attention to the US Congress."[74]

In an article in its November–December 1970 newsletter, the NASSP informed its members of its resolve in a front-page story, "NASSP Hits Displacement of Principals," that detailed the chronology of correspondence with the Attorney General. "If the Department [of Justice] fails to initiate strong action," the organization promised, "NASSP will aggressively persist in its efforts to ameliorate the situation."[75]

And thus the fight continued.

5

SUPERINTENDENTS, THE SOUTHERN MANIFESTO, AND SCHOOL CHOICE

It is not intemperate to state that, at this time, as fast as we desegregate schools, we eliminate Black principals. The pattern is clear and inexorable.

—J. C. Banks, *The New Republic*, September 24, 1970

Discrimination is rampant in the name of desegregation.

—Benjamin E. Mays, President, Morehouse College
Atlanta Daily World, August 27, 1971

IT WAS NO WONDER that Black principals and teachers were being fired, demoted, and displaced altogether. Despite the 1954 *Brown* decision, White superintendents and school boards acted with impunity as they defied the law of the land by resisting the integration of Black students and school personnel. In this regard, local superintendents and school boards were in sync with their national associations, the American Association of School Administrators (AASA) and the National School Board Association, which were founded in 1866 and 1940, respectively. By the time the *Brown* decision came down, each organization had a solid record of holding national convenings, issuing resolutions on national and international education issues, and providing professional development. Yet neither organization supported the *Brown* decision. In fact, superintendents and boards did little to lead communities toward integration. Rather, they reflected an antagonism toward desegregation and used the language of "state rights," "local and state control," and "moderation" to cloak their open defiance of the law. The superintendents' fight was so pervasive and drawn out that Judge John Minor Wisdom of the US Court of Appeals for the Fifth Circuit—a prominent southern judge and consistent proponent of desegregation across all aspects of American life—pointed out that segregated schools were created by school boards in their administration of school districts and not exclusively by dual school systems decreed by their legislatures. In pushing school officials to desegregate Wisdom advanced the notion that a "right without an effective remedy is meaningless" when he declared "The only school desegregation plan that meets constitutional standards is one that works."[1]

In 1963, Dr. Martin Luther King, Jr., described Alabama's Governor George Wallace "having his lips dripping with the words of interposition and nullification." Opposition to *Brown* was so virulent that Dr. King's observation did not apply only to Wallace, who infamously proclaimed "Segregation now, tomorrow, and forever," in his gubernatorial inauguration speech. It also described the actions of White superintendents, school boards, and local citizens. In fact, though both concepts were constitutionally illegitimate, interposition (the right of the states to protect their interests from federal violations deemed by the states to be dangerous or unconstitutional) and nullification (the theory that a state can invalidate a federal law it considers unconstitutional) proved useful tools in the decades-long warfare against *Brown*.

SUPERINTENDENTS AND SCHOOL BOARDS DEFY *BROWN*

On February 14, 1953, the executive committee of the AASA met in Atlantic City, New Jersey, where they discussed *Brown* and arrived at an unconscionable decision: *to do nothing*. The executive committee minutes record this discussion:

> *Supreme Court Decision on Segregation*—The committee discussed what the Association should do following the Supreme Court decision on segregation and what the attitude of the Association should be. Secretary McClure reported that the Association had avoided saying anything about the matter and had scheduled nothing on the 1954 convention program discussing the segregation issue, because any such discussion might be viewed as an attempt to influence the decision.

The AASA's executive committee kept its word: nothing appeared on its convention program that year about the most momentous decision in American education in the twentieth century. In June 1954, the group's newsletter,

School Administrator, ran a front-page column urging gradualism and postponement, under the banner "The Court's Decision on Segregation Calls for Cool Heads, Wise Leadership." The September 1954 school year opened without the AASA providing any decision-affirming guidance to its members about how to desegregate schools.

By October 1954, the AASA announced record membership growth had tripled, reaching some nine thousand members. That same year, the organization selected Henry J. Willett, the White superintendent of Richmond (Virginia) Public Schools, as president-elect who served as president from 1955–1956. During this same period, Virginia's governor, Thomas B. Stanley, declared integration "a cancer eating at the very lifeblood of our public school system" and supported US Senator Harry F. Byrd, who had helped author the "Southern Manifesto" and devised the "Massive Resistance" strategy. Both the Manifesto and Massive Resistance mobilized White politicians and White citizens to stop public school desegregation. Virginia "in length and level of resistance became more like the deep South as time went by";[2] and AASA President Willett, like many of his superintendent peers, did not support integration early-on. In fact, in describing Willett, Henry L. Marsh (one of the civil rights attorneys who fought Virginia's massive resistance strategy) stated "no superintendent actively supported integration. They reflected the views of their board."[3]

The November 1954 AASA annual conference proceeded as if *Brown* had never occurred, with a conference agenda highlighting topics such as Social Security for superintendents, exhibits at regional conferences, and school construction.

More than a year after the *Brown* decision, AASA finally provided a perspective to its members about desegregation. The September 1955 issue of the *School Administrator* featured an article about Chattanooga, Tennessee, being a model for school desegregation. Under the misleading headline "Chattanooga Board Takes Positive Stand on Segregation Issue," the newsletter commended Chattanooga's board of education decision not to desegregate immediately and called the board's statement about its position "moderate, dignified, and well-phrased," when it was actually open defiance of the law. In fact, according to the article, the school board plainly publicized in a letter to Chattanoogans, "Your school board does not plan to integrate our schools by September 1955" and went on to say that it would "counsel with the people of our community seeking their advice and opinions."

By the following school year, AASA's executive committees and the membership endorsed a decision at the annual meeting to oppose *Brown*, summarizing their perspective by stating that they "wisely believed that this is an issue to be resolved at local and state levels."

DESIGNING SCHEMES: USING STATE LAWS AND TAX DOLLARS TO UNDO *BROWN*

AASA's leaders and members mimicked the type of recalcitrant resistance of the law that was typical of White southern officials and citizens who claimed that the federal government's actions intruded on states' rights—when, in fact, the US Constitution's Supremacy Clause clearly requires state laws to yield to conflicting federal laws.

Well into the mid-1970s—nearly two decades after the *Brown* decision became the law of the land—the South and all of its White-controlled mechanisms of government, including courts, police forces, superintendents, school boards, mayors, and city councils, engaged in an outright fight against equal educational opportunity for Black boys and girls. White control of all the levers of public spaces continued as before, even though Blacks paid federal and state taxes to support the public schools, public libraries, and public buses to which they had limited or no access. When faced with the *Brown* decision, White school boards, superintendents, and citizens purposely resisted the new law of the land, often going to extremes to maintain and perpetuate White control of the nation's public schools.

Over time, those extremes worked—and they worked well. Operating under the guise of mainstream policymaking, White extremists' efforts deliberately prevented implementation of the 1954 *Brown* decision by more than twenty years.

But the reality is that when *Brown* first became law, the nation had a choice: desegregate schools by integrating Black principals and teachers along with Black students, or fight desegregation of schools every step of the way and with extreme measures. Obviously, the latter course was chosen, a course evident in decades of court decisions and open, protracted, and sustained hostility to *Brown* by untold numbers of White elected officials, school district leaders, and citizens. Many southern states went so far as to amend their constitutions and use state tax dollars to fund *Brown*'s delay and their racial animus. Some school districts even closed their schools for an entire academic year or more rather than desegregate. Never mind that such actions essentially vacated the state's responsibility to provide a free and compulsory education to its children and youth and left both Black and White students unschooled.

The state of Mississippi, for one, took the brazen approach of establishing a State Sovereignty Commission to "protect the sovereignty of the State of Mississippi and her sister states" and prevent the federal government from enforcing school desegregation mandates.[4] The Sovereignty Commission was composed of twelve members appointed by the governor and ex officio members including the lieutenant governor, the speaker of the House of Representatives, and the attorney general. On its establishment, the Commission was budgeted $250,000. One of its enforcement arms was the Citizen's Council, a White supremacist organization devised to terrorize supporters of desegregation and voting rights. From 1960 to 1964, the Citizen's Council received funding from the Commission totaling more than $190,000.

Another unashamed act of defiance was the southern states' creation and support of hundreds of small, segregated private schools ("seg academies"), many funded by state tax dollars. As Black schools were closed in the name of desegregation, personnel and other funds that supported them were diverted and used to provide vouchers, tuition grants, and financial aid to a growing system of all-White private schools. This practice was labelled a "voluntary desegregation plan of school choice." It was not until January 31, 1969, that Mississippi's practice of this kind of "school choice" was ruled unconstitutional. Just four years earlier, in 1965, the NAACP had taken on a similar case that knocked down the state's "grade-a-year freedom of choice plan" when Black parents argued that under the plan, desegregation of schools would be delayed until 1976—a full twenty-two years (and almost two generations of schoolchildren) after *Brown*. In fact, it was not until 1970, when the *Singleton v. Jackson Municipal Separate School District* case was settled, that a unitary school system with desegregated facilities was achieved in Mississippi.

Speaking ten years after *Brown* in *Atlantic Monthly*, Dr. Martin Luther King, Jr., condemned the lack of progress on desegregation, saying "Negro school children [are] still victimized by the crippling chains of segregated schools." He especially castigated the city of Atlanta and the state of Mississippi, calling the lack of progress shameful and appalling:

> The naive might believe that great strides have been made in school desegregation over the past decade, but this is not at all true . . . Today, the

> tragically real picture of school desegregation, particularly in the South, is still one of stark tokenism or no desegregation at all. In my own hometown of Atlanta, for example, the awful truth is that of 14,159 Negroes enrolled in high schools, only 153 are presently attending classes with Whites, and, worse, not a single Negro child attends a desegregated elementary school. The pattern is the same all over the deep South, and those states which have moved at all in any effort to comply with the Supreme Court's decision have done so with a gradualism and tokenism that is shamefully appalling.[5]

Of course, King was right, but the ultimate stall tactic involved changing state laws and statutes and diverting state tax dollars to confound and stymie *Brown*. These tactics were not unique to Mississippi or Georgia. And they really amounted to nothing more than schemes cropping up all across the dual-system states. The schemes were explicitly designed to keep White students, teachers, and principals from sharing school buildings with Blacks and prevent the equalization of fiscal resources that flowed to schools serving Black students. The schemes were called school choice plans, vouchers, tuition grants, and financial aid—and each enacted financial equations to benefit Whites. Each of these schemes well served its intended purpose.

WHAT BECAME OF THE SENATE HEARINGS

For all practical purposes, compliance with *Brown* was soon to be almost exclusively actualized as the act of placing Black students in previously all-White schools. The goal and court mandates requiring that districts integrate school administration and faculties would be abandoned. Nevertheless, the Senate hearings had not been held in vain. The testimonies and copious data highlighted and confirmed that without Black principals and teachers, school desegregation could not and had not been achieved—even nearly two decades after *Brown*. Going into the 1970s, remedy was still needed.

The June 14, 1971, session of Senate hearings concluded at 11:45 a.m. with a statement by NASSP attorney Thomas William George. Though this national organization of principals was largely White in membership, Black principals nonetheless succeeded in galvanizing its attention and support. Of all the majority-White professional education associations in the US at the time, the NASSP was the Black educator's fiercest ally.

"The critical issue before this Senate committee today" proclaimed George, "is the status of another vanishing American, the Black principal." In his testimony, George attributed the displacement problem to "catastrophic discrimination" and cautioned that "time was running out to arrest the degradation and humiliation being suffered" by Black principals.[6] To underscore his and NASSP's conviction about this issue, George entered into the final Senate hearing record a report by J. C. James, Chief of the Operations Review Branch of HEW. James had compiled his report statistics while working as a Federal Executive Fellow at the Brookings Institution when he was on leave from his post as a Howard University associate dean of admissions. According to James, Black principals represented an "avenue of understanding, guidance and communication" essential to the progress of a multiracial America. In his view, the nation could not "fail in its challenge to give its youth the opportunity for contacts and learning experiences through interaction with leadership from all ethnic groups."[7]

As the plight of Black principals became more widely known across the nation, many other public figures weighed in on what the demise of these influential Black leaders meant for the pipeline of future Black educators, excellence in public education delivery, the ideals of American democracy, and children's development. Black author and activist Zora Neale Hurston asserted as early as 1955, in a guest opinion piece for the *Orlando Sentinel*, that the removal of Black teachers after *Brown* was an affront to equality: "It is a contradiction in terms to scream . . . equality while at the same time spurning Negro teachers." Other Black intellectuals wrote about the impact of removing Black leaders from schools and what their absence would mean to children. "This distorted image of the Negro has its negative effect on children too," wrote the essayist John Oliver Killens. "It gives them a distorted image of this earth and of human potential and ill equips them to live in a world three-quarters of which is colored and fast becoming independent and free."

Samuel Ethridge, executive secretary to the NEA, echoed these concerns in a June 16, 1971, letter to Senator Walter Mondale, the chair of the Senate hearings. "What happens to Black and White children who see no Black leadership?" he asked. "It gives these students a 'distorted image of Blacks.'"[8]

Like those before him, Ethridge was determined to communicate the message that the Black principal was the southern Black community's highest public official. He argued that to "downgrade [the principal] was to downgrade the Black community."[9] And he was right. Black principals were active and essential civic leaders. They worked with the NAACP to open local chapters, led worker and voting rights campaigns, controlled financial resources (though often meager), allocated a broad ecosystem of jobs related to the operation of their schools (including secretaries, bus drivers, and groundskeepers), and collaborated with HBCU college presidents and professors to advance students' higher education aspirations. With this slate of responsibilities and visibility, Ethridge believed that Black principals "reaffirmed Black success as an attainable goal in America." Furthermore, their demise "dramatically violated" young Blacks' belief in the American dream.[10]

In fact, when Blacks were removed from the principalship and replaced by Whites, Black principals, teachers, and students suffered the same fate, according to an NEA March 1970 report: "submersion of their interest and identities" and decimation of "every symbol of Black identity."[11] With the decimation of Black principals and teachers came the elimination of Black school buildings named for Black notables of national and local significance, as well as disregard for all awards and trophies earned by Black students for state and district science fairs, oratory contests, and athletic competitions—leaving a painful void and a negative (and erroneous) impression in integrated schools that Black principals, teachers, and students had achieved nothing of note or record prior to entering the new, integrated schools. Ethridge warned that unless "something is done to reshape the attitudes of superintendents and boards toward Negro administrators, we are going to lose a lot of the talent and leadership that we already have."[12]

Unfortunately, the Senate Select Committee's dispiriting conclusion was that "the leadership role in the community as exerted by the Black administrator is now lost." The fallout from this loss was that Black educators' "influence and representation on the policy level is now diminished . . . This seems to be another phase of the price the Black student must pay in the desegregation process."[13]

With the last words, "Regardless of what is being done, the ranks of the Black principal in the South are being depleted," the Senate Select Committee on Equal Educational Opportunity adjourned on June 14, 1971, and set to reconvene the next day.

The next day, the Senate Select Committee reconvened at 10:00 a.m. with opening testimony from the NAACP. The NAACP spokesperson reminded the Senators that the Supreme Court had made clear that "in implementing desegregation plans, district courts and school officials were required to consider not only student assignments but all other aspects of school operations, including teachers and other school personnel."[14] Of course, this integration of Black princpals and teachers into desegregating schools was not happening. Julius Chambers of the NAACP Legal Defense Fund was the first to testify that morning. Chambers had successfully litigated the *Swann v. Charlotte-Mecklenburg Board of Education* decision before the US Supreme Court. The 1971 *Swann* decision upheld busing programs as a mechanism for speeding up racial integration of public schools. On the matter of helping rectify the illegal treatment of Black principals, however, Chambers stated that the Department of Justice and HEW had been of no help and "showed no interest in getting into challenging practices of discrimination within integrated or racially mixed schools."[15] Although he chaired the committee and rarely interjected, Senator Mondale observed at this point, "It is my opinion that the Justice Department wishes to pursue a policy of non-law enforcement."[16]

And so, on that day—June 15, 1971—the Committee's attention turned away from faculty and administration desegregation to debates about busing, pairing and clustering of schools for racial balance, school attendance areas to promote integration of schools, and the duty of school officials in de facto segregated schools to desegregate. The discussion of desegregation and integration now focused exclusively on mechanisms to achieve racial balance in student populations.

Paradoxically, the strategy to remedy the decimation of Black principals and teachers dried up just as Black students entered desegregated schools. Thus, desegregated schools remained all-White in their leadership, teaching force, curriculum and culture, and most important, the policymaking levers that controlled them. In his remarks before the Senate Select Committee, Senator George McGovern of South Dakota concluded that this reality was deleterious to the goals and intent of *Brown*. "The plight of Black school officials," Senator McGovern said, "symbolizes the incomplete implementation of the *Brown v. Board of Education* decision. We had expected that the demand for qualified Black educators would increase as a result of this decision. Instead, they have found themselves pushed out of responsible positions which would have given them administrative responsibility for both Black and White students."[17]

Despite earlier court orders, there were to be no plans for racially balancing the principal and teacher ranks in desegregated schools. The NEA's *amicus* brief submitted for the Senate hearings concluded sharply: "As the dual systems were ordered to a close, the job security from Black educators inhering in those systems vanished."[18]

6

IMPLEMENTING *BROWN* WITHOUT BLACK PRINCIPALS AND TEACHERS

The nation can ill afford a future in which White and minority children see exclusively White authority figures in their schools.

—The Carnegie Forum on Education and the Economy, 1986

The statistical data showing the elimination of Black educators in this Circuit demonstrates that further remedial action is necessary to preserve the rights of school children to a desegregated education [and to] protect Black educators from discriminatory personnel policies . . .

— National Education Association, 1971

THE "DELAY IN implementing *Brown* was the refuge of racism," declared Senator George McGovern of South Dakota before the Senate Select Committee in 1971. In this statement, McGovern echoed the conclusions of the National Advisory Commission on Civil Disorders in a 1968 report about desegregation: "The single most persuasive and abrasive element in America life, tearing at the fabric of our society, is the element of White racism."[1] It was clear that this "abrasive element" was inflicting trauma.

A COMMUNITY-WIDE TRAUMA

By the late 1970s, White resistance—or rather, White racism—had systematically and ruthlessly decimated the ranks of Black principals and teachers in reconfigured unitary school systems across the South. In this annihilation, the nation lost at least 100,000 Black principals and teachers.

As ample documentation at the 1971 Senate hearings confirmed, the historical record shows that the Black principals and teachers who were demoted and fired were—in nearly every single case and in every one of the seventeen dual-system states—replaced by Whites who were far less academically credentialed and professionally experienced. In this purge, the nation lost thousands of its most highly trained educators. They were never replaced.

In fact, as student enrollment swelled in desegregating schools due to the enrollment of newly integrated Black students, school districts scrambled to hire more White principals and White teachers to meet the demand. With Black principals and teachers out of the picture, and with no intention to hire or rehire them to meet the growing need, White school boards and superintendents quickly devised fast tracks into the principalship and teaching for Whites. The invention of teacher shortages and alternative certification routes became popular tools to quickly populate schools and classrooms with White adults.

In observing this phenomenon throughout the state of Tennessee and elsewhere, C. C. Bond, an assistant superintendent for Chattanooga Public Schools, noted that emergency certificates were being issued by school authorities for employment of White teachers who had not completed basic academic requirements, such as a bachelor's degree from an accredited college. Thurgood Marshall, then an attorney for the NAACP's Legal Defense and Educational Fund, also found this same disturbing trend, reporting what he believed to be the most egregious case he had ever encountered—in rural Georgia, the replacement of a Black teacher with bachelor's and master's degrees by a White milkman.

Yet there was no shortage of qualified and certified Black principals and teachers in the years leading up to and after *Brown*. In every one of the seventeen state-by-state reports submitted to the 1971 Senate Hearings, as well as in field reports filed by the American Federation of Teachers, the National Education Association, and the National Association of Secondary School Principals, and in data cited by numerous court cases, Black principals and teachers were found to have academic credentials, certification levels, and years of professional experience that exceeded White educators generally, and those who replaced them specifically.

In a blatant homage to Jim Crow, traditional ascension patterns to the principalship and teaching ranks went out the door. Now, in addition to White educators, Whites who had been unemployed, local shopkeepers, athletic league coaches, mail carriers, and some working-class laborers—usually White men—were offered an open door to educator positions. At times, it appeared that any White warm body would do, so that Black principals would not lead in schools with White teachers and Black teachers would not teach in schools with White children. Particularly hard-hit were Black men, who comprised most of the Black school principalships that were wiped out.

Dr. Benjamin E. Mays, the iconic civil rights leader who was mentor to Dr. Martin Luther King, Jr., president of Morehouse College, and an Atlanta Public Schools Board member, characterized the annihilation of Black principals and teachers as traumatic. The trauma that resulted from White racist resistance to *Brown* was at least fourfold: a decline in the economic and political power of southern Blacks; a reduction in the caliber of public school leadership for the South; a dampening of the professional aspirations of Black educators; and measurable harm to the intellectual and social development and well-being of Black youth.

The first trauma was economic. Before the *Brown* decision in 1954, nearly half of all Black professionals were teachers, compared with less than 25 percent of White professionals. Some have argued that the elimination of Black leadership in education is not quantifiable. However, ostensible inability to quantify an effect does not necessarily mean there is no effect. Indeed, the Black community *felt* the loss of economic and political power, the loss of leadership symbols, the loss of success symbols, and the loss of symbols of aspiration. The names were known. Many, but by no means all, are listed in the hundreds of pages in the 1971 Senate hearing transcripts. Those men and women counted.

On the economic front, the lowest estimates calculated the financial loss to be about $250 million for elimination of 30,000 Black educator jobs. The numbers grew through the years to at least 100,000 Black principals and teachers shunted off payrolls. Over time, desegregation left southern Black educators nearly $1 billion poorer.

According to Vernon E. Jordan, then president of the National Urban League, a total of 23,000 new principal and teaching jobs were created in eleven southeastern states between 1968 and 1971. Blacks were placed in fewer than 500 of these new jobs. White hires happened at the economic expense of Black educators, resulting in White economic gains that continue today.

The second trauma was equally distressing: namely, the damage done to school systems because of the loss of high-caliber leadership. Proven Black leaders were replaced on a near one-to-one basis with Whites who held lesser or no qualifications. The Black professionals remaining in the system were made answerable to less-qualified Whites or placed in federally funded jobs that were subject to discontinuation when funding ceased. This immense brain drain yielded school systems led not by experts in the field, but by racist fearmongers maneuvering and manipulating the system to maintain White power and jobs at the expense of Black educators and children.

The assault on the professional identity and stature of Black educators ensured that the "desegregated" school system would be held captive by the same Jim Crow power structure that had fought vehemently against desegregation for decades. As journalist Paul Ryan put it, writing for the *Chicago Daily Defender* about school systems in Louisiana and Mississippi, the South's desegregating schools "operated on terms and conditions set by Whites, governed by White values, attitudes and traditions," and "preoccupied with the myth of White supremacy."[2]

The third trauma resulted from the "near total disintegration of Black authority in every area of public education" and the destruction of the aspirations of Black educators and young people.[3] Mindful of the notoriety and leadership enjoyed by Blacks in the community prior to *Brown*, it is not unreasonable to assume that the next generation of Black youth, observing the fate of their elders, would worry that they would have limited futures as principals and teachers. On this matter, a 1972 NEA report concluded that Black people's very survival necessitated the identification and promotion of a new generation of Black educators, who should have productive career options restored.

The fourth trauma was the unkindest cut of all. If schooling is about the children, as all the sentimental slogans profess, Black children did not seem to count. The well-being of Black children was not part of the consideration or calculation as schools desegregated and purged Black educators. Shunted into "new" schools without Black models of authority who could also serve as guides and protectors, Black students were subjected to physical violence and emotional abuse, racial intimidation and hostility, and illegal suspensions.

The effect of the loss of Black educators on Black students did not go unrecognized. Even the US Commissioner of Education and *Time* magazine drew attention to the issue, in a June 18, 1965, article titled "Teachers: Segregation by Integration." Commissioner Francis Keppel worried about the loss of Black educators and what it meant for Black and White students' identities and democracy's future. "We must not deceive ourselves that the exclusion of Negroes is not noticed by children," he told *Time*. "What can they assume but that Negroes are not deemed by the community as worthy of a place in mixed classrooms? What can the White child assume but that he is somehow special and exclusive, protected from some sort of contamination? How can the world of democracy have meaning to such children?"[4]

ASSESSING THE DAMAGE DONE

Even US President Dwight Eisenhower, who signed the Civil Rights Act of 1957 and sent Army troops to enforce integration of the Little Rock, Arkansas, public schools, was unable to imagine the extent and degree of the resistance that would play out over the ensuing decades. In December 1954, he wrote in private correspondence to a family friend, "The segregation issue will, I think become acute or tend to die out according to the character of the procedure orders that the Court will probably issue this winter. My own guess is that they will be very moderate and accord a maximum of initiative to local courts."

Like many others on the forefront of this fight, Eisenhower underestimated the massive resistance of southern Whites to integration. The combined effects of deliberate underpayment of Black principals and teachers and differentiated pay scales for Black and White educators; amended state constitutions; statewide school closings to avoid desegregation; suspension of tax levies for public schools; decimation of the Black principal and teacher pipelines; redirection of state tax dollars to Whites' "school choice" vouchers and segregation academies; and the establishment of segregated classrooms and academic tracking—all these factors were deliberate, directed means to a disinvestment in the education of Black students.

With Black educators out of the way, nominal levels of desegregation were attempted—but true integration of America's schools has never occurred. With help from Black Americans' (and democracy's) old nemesis, Jim Crow, the nation's public school systems have been left without the knowledge, skills, and democratic activism of an exceptional cadre of Black educational leadership. Put bluntly, schools nationwide were left with a less talented cohort of educators. In the end, White resistance to *Brown* resulted in maintenance of White-controlled public schools. Despite more than fifty judicial rulings that attempted to ensure democratic participation in school governance, the White power structure maintained control of superintendencies, school boards, and formulation of school funding mechanisms. This Jim Crow–inspired White establishment ensured that the desegregated schools were White-controlled spaces in terms of instructional delivery, curriculum authorship and content, school culture, and educational policy and practice.

Left behind were knowledgeable school leaders who could have shaped district policies and practices to make real the ideal of integrated schools. Left behind was the prospect of schools that would reflect the science of teaching and learning that Black educators had gained in their HBCU teacher education programs and in their master's and doctoral programs at elite northern universities (because they were locked out of universities in their own states).

Where the thousands of displaced Black educators went, no one really knows for sure, but scant records indicate that older Black principals and teachers went into involuntary early retirement. Some remained in the "integrated system" serving under less-qualified Whites. Some maintained positions in federal desegregation programs until the "soft money" ran out. Some joined HBCUs as education faculty and administrators. Others found jobs outside of education, if at all. Many who suffered from derailed careers were unable to transcend the circumstances or go elsewhere.

Furthermore, the widespread displacement of educators during these years has been documented to have dissuaded an entire next generation of young Black people from entering the teaching profession in the first place. In the years immediately prior to *Brown*, Blacks enrolled in teacher education programs in record numbers, but soon afterward, Blacks grew wary of their futures in the profession. Frank B. Belk, placement director for Shaw University in North Carolina, told the 1971 Senate committee that Black teacher education graduates were "growing suspicious of the teaching profession and its predominantly White administrators" and stated, "The bigots, they're grinning and saying come on in and closing the door at the same time."[5]

On the heels of *Brown*, schools were no longer safe spaces for Black children's unabated intellectual growth and psychological well-being. No longer could Black children find schools peopled with Black principals and teachers who could reach, teach, inspire, and protect them from the treachery and violence of racism and teach them strategies for achieving excellence in the face of White racism. The absence of Black principals and teachers illustrated the sad reality that desegregated schools would reflect a belief in the intellectual and cultural inferiority of Blacks and actualize a consistent antipathy to Black educational leadership, particularly regarding policy formulation and funding.

In the wake of desegregation, massive Black student suspensions occurred as Black student protested violent and unequal treatment in integrated schools. A 1972 NEA report covering eleven southern states counted 12,111 student walkouts, boycotts or demonstrations; 11,146 suspensions and expulsions; 2,000 arrests; and in Mississippi alone, 22,750 students expelled from school.

Schools that would fairly embrace all children and honor their intellectual abilities and talents, unrestricted by skin color—the prospect of having such schools was left behind as an entire workforce of highly qualified, experienced Black educators were systematically locked out of America's schools.

7

THE PAST IS EVER PRESENT

Living in a world restricted by laws defining race, as well as creating obstacles, disadvantages, and even superstitions regarding race, challenged my capacity for survival. For ninety years I have witnessed countless men and women likewise meet this challenge.

—John Hope Franklin
James E. Duke Professor Emeritus of History
Mirror to America, 2005

Many good Black administrators are being dismissed from schools that would have much stronger systems if they were retained.

—B. F. Lever, Coordinator
Arkansas Department of Education, 1970

THE CLOCK ON *Brown* did not begin in 1954. In many ways that clock did not begin until the mid-1970s. Today, fifty years into its actual implementation, the nation is still reeling from the fallout associated with the decimation of Black principals and teachers—the largest brain drain of expertise and talent ever experienced in the US public school system (or perhaps any nation's education system). Prior to *Brown*, Black principals and teachers comprised 35 percent to 50 percent of the educator workforce in the seventeen dual-system states. Nearly seventy years later, in 2021, no state begins to approach those percentages. The cumulative effect of consistent and broad discriminatory practices resulted in a purging of a superior national resource that has yet to be replaced.

THE EDUCATOR WORKFORCE AFTER *BROWN*

There is a direct line from the past to the present. And the past is not yet past. The decline in Black principal and teacher production and appointments continues. Data from the National Principal and Teacher Survey of 2017–2018, compiled by the National Center for Education Statistics (NCES) and published in 2020, provides a revealing picture of the nation's educator workforce:

- Today, the nation's schools have 93,200 principals, only 11 percent of them Black.
- Of the nation's 3.2 million teachers, only 7 percent are Black.
- Notably, nearly 70 percent of principals and teachers in urban schools with a predominantly Black student body are White, making the current generation of Black students the largest ever to have no access to Black models of intellectual authority and educational leadership.
- Fewer than 3 percent of the nation's 13,800 school districts are led by Black superintendents.

These low numbers persist, even though Black principals and teachers, then and now, are the nation's most academically credentialed and professionally experienced educators. Much like those who preceded them, today's Black principals and teachers are more likely to hold a doctoral degree than their White peers. Among Black principals, 21.5 percent hold a doctorate, compared with 9.2 percent of White principals. As a group, Black principals also tend to have more years of experience as classroom teachers when they ascend to the principalship than their White peers.

Among Black teachers, 2.1 percent hold the doctoral degree as their highest degree, compared with 1.0 percent of White teachers. Almost half (49.2 percent) of the nation's teaching force and 61 percent of principals hold a master's degree as their highest degree. White males hold a master's degree as the highest degree attained at higher percentages than any other group, a finding that suggests that they are able to attain principalships, central office directorships, and superintendencies with fewer or lower academic credentials than Black men, Black women, or White women.

An analysis of the 2017–2018 NCES data shows that when the academic credentials of Black women, Black men, White women, and White men who serve as principals and teachers are compared with one another, Black women and Black men come out at the top. Among Black female principals, nearly 50 percent hold a degree higher than a master's degree. Slightly more than 40 percent of Black male principals hold a degree higher than a master's degree. White female principals follow Black men, with 38.2 percent holding a degree higher than a master's degree. White male principals are the least academically credentialed in comparison with all groups, with 35.8 percent holding a degree higher than the master's degree.

A similar pattern holds true for highest academic degrees held for teachers. Among Black female teachers, 14.5 percent hold the highest degree, followed by 9.8 percent of Black male teachers, 8.8 percent of White female teachers, and 7 percent of White male teachers. (See table 7.1.)

Given these data about Black educators, why are they underrepresented in critical school district policy and leadership posts such as the principalship and superintendency? The data show that less-credentialed and less-experienced Whites (particularly White males) hold these posts in percentages that far exceed their representation in the teacher workforce—the traditional source for growing and recruiting principals and superintendents.

The answers to this question lie in the painful history of segregation and racial discrimination. First, the underrepresentation of Blacks in the principalship and teaching force is rooted in the history of aggressive firings and demotions of Black educators after *Brown*. These displacements were the result of White racism and exclusive control (enforced by segregationist laws) of the levers of local governance that excluded Blacks from superintendent appointments, school board elections, and school funding decisions. This assault on Black educational leadership not only affected the immediate

TABLE 7.1 Public school principals and teachers by race/sex and highest degree earned

	PERCENTAGE OF PUBLIC SCHOOL PRINCIPALS HOLDING HIGHER THAN A MASTER'S DEGREE*	PERCENTAGE OF PUBLIC SCHOOL TEACHERS HOLDING HIGHER THAN A MASTER'S DEGREE*
Race/sex		
Black females	48.4	14.5
Black males	40.3	9.8
White females	38.2	8.8
White males	35.8	7.0

Source: National Center for Education Statistics (NCES), 2020, based on National Principal and Teacher Survey (NPTS), 2017–2018.

**Higher than a master's degree* includes doctorate, education specialist, and certificate of advanced studies.

generation of educators who were dismissed, but also profoundly displaced, and in too many cases extinguished, the interests of a future generation of Black educators.

Second, though education is a notoriously female-friendly field, notions about who should lead still tend to support White males' access to policy and leadership posts. Despite some changes, school leadership remains nearly as monolithic as it was forty years ago, when Harry F. Walcott wrote the ethnographic study *The Man in the Principal's Office*.[1] Today, approximately 70 percent of public school superintendents, central office associate superintendents, directors, and principals are White males. Yet White males make up less than 16 percent of the nation's teaching force and tend to be less academically credentialed than their Black male and female peers.

THE IMPACT OF BLACK EDUCATORS ON STUDENT ACHIEVEMENT

More than forty years of research exists about the impact Black teachers have on Black students' academic achievement and education attainment. This research does not advocate for race-matching of students. However, it does elucidate the academic and social benefits that accrue to Black students who are in desegregated schools with higher percentages of Black teachers and/or assigned to Black teachers. In these settings, Black students are:

- More likely to graduate from high school
- More likely to be tested for and placed in gifted and talented programs
- Less likely to be misplaced in special education classes
- More likely to be described as "intellectually capable"
- More likely to engage in positive school behaviors such as completing homework, attending school regularly, and serving in leadership roles
- Less likely to be suspended or expelled[2]

Specifically, quantitative studies dating back to the 1990s have found that Black teachers express higher expectations for Black students' academic and social behaviors and achieve more beneficial outcomes than White teachers do with Black students.[3] Black teachers positively influence Black students' school attendance; increase reading comprehension and vocabulary scores on standardized tests; increase college matriculation rates; and increase enrollment in Algebra II, a course required for college entrance.[4] A Vanderbilt University study found that Black students are three times more likely to be assigned to gifted programs when taught by a Black teacher than a non-Black teacher, and that high-achieving Black students who are taught by Black teachers have gifted program assignment rates similar to high-achieving White students.[5]

"The Long-Run Impacts of Same Race Teachers," a 2018 study conducted by researchers at Johns Hopkins University, University of California, Davis, and American University and disseminated by the National Bureau of Economic Research, found that Black students who have one Black teacher by the third grade are 13 percent more likely to enroll in college. If they have two Black teachers, they are 32 percent more likely to enroll. Notably, the researchers found having at least one Black teacher in elementary school reduced Black students' probability of dropping out by 29 percent for low-income Black students overall, and by 39 percent for low-income Black boys in particular. In explaining their findings about the differential impact of Black teachers, the researchers found a clear causal link between Black students being assigned a Black teacher and the likelihood of graduating from high school and going on to college. Black students were "7 percent more likely to graduate high school and 4 percent more likely to enroll in college than their peers who were not assigned to Black teachers."[6] Further, the researchers cited both a role-modeling effect and Black teachers' professional experiences. On the role-modeling effect, they concluded that Black teachers provided a vital counterpoint to preexisting beliefs about Black achievement: "For students facing aspirations gaps due to limited information on what is possible, a Black teacher provides an effective counterexample that causes them to update their priors and change their beliefs, effort, and trajectories."[7]

Regarding Black teachers' professional experiences, the NBER researchers concluded that Black teachers are more experienced, may be better teachers than Whites, and explicitly addressed affective factors tied to learning and academic achievement:

> One possible explanation of our results is that the Black teachers in the schools and classrooms serving Black students are simply better teachers than their White counterparts. Indeed, the summary statistics presented . . . show that Black teachers had about 3 more years of experience than White teachers, on average.

> Foster (1990, 1997) explicitly introduced the concept of teaching a non-academic hidden curriculum, which includes self-esteem and pride in your racial identity; cultural solidarity, affiliation, and connectedness with the larger Black community; and the unique (to Black students) political and social reasons for educational attainment.[8]

This contemporary research about teachers' effects on students underscores the fact that the forced exodus of Black teachers after *Brown* left Black students without teachers who could or would teach self-esteem tied to an appropriate pride in racial history and cultural accomplishments; likewise, Black students now had few teachers who modeled the importance of educational attainment and its tie to broader Black uplift and empowerment. There is evidence that Black students in segregated schools took pride in the academic accomplishments of their teachers. The October 25, 1946, issue of the all-Black Sumner High School newspaper (the *Sumner Courier*) ran two short articles about teachers who earned their master's degrees—romance languages teacher Vera Jackson Reynolds, who earned a master's degree in French from the University of Kansas, and the Constitution teacher and athletic coach J. L. Thatcher, who earned a master's degree with a concentration in economics from Colorado University (now University of Colorado, Boulder). The articles also referenced Reynolds's and Jackson's master's thesis titles: "Renee Maran, Spokesman for Africa" and "Recent Trends in State and Local Government," respectively.[9]

Black children, like Black adults, are required daily to negotiate social, economic, and political structures that engage them first (and sometimes, always) as Black. In these transactions, "Black" is operationalized by the White-controlled power structure as a deficit and danger. But Black teachers can stand in opposition to the notion of Black as a deficit. Black educators have life experiences and the ability to serve as "cultural intercessors and translators" for Black students.[10] Additionally, for all children, their presence as the intellectual authority figure in the classroom can help upend racist stereotypes about intellectual inferiority among Blacks.

Research is also beginning to show that Black principals have positive effects on Black students' academic achievement and attainment that are similar to those of Black teachers. The role-modeling effect pertains to Black principals' impact on Black students. An illustration of this effect appears in a 2001 ethnographic case study about an Atlanta, Georgia, high school led by a Black male principal. In this study, *Keeping a Close Watch: A Cultural Philosophy of School Change*, Carter and Fenwick found that the presence of a Black male principal, administrative staff, and teachers helped undo the multiple negative stereotypes about Black people held by Black students.[11]

The study observes how the principal led in a way that purposely sought to have students experience Black educators who were positive and supportive, because he believed that such exposure would spur academic achievement. Teachers described the principal as a "counselor at heart" whom students didn't see as "a jailer." Teachers experienced him as a facilitator—ensuring and gathering needed resources so that they could reach and teach their students. Students viewed the principal as a trusted father figure.

The principal went about creating an academically rigorous and nurturing environment by explicitly recruiting Black men with doctoral degrees to the high school's leadership team and faculty. He purposely deviated from the typical pattern of appointing Black men as coaches and disciplinarians and instead appointed them as assistant principals, guidance counselors, teachers, and the director of technology.

The researchers found that students viewed the men's presence in their school as unusual and positive. Additionally, students were clearly able to express the impact these administrators and teachers had on their ideas about Black people generally, and Black men specifically. "That was one of the first things I noticed when I came here," said one student. "When I watch TV, everyone says Black men are in jail, doing drugs, fighting each other. But when I come to school, I see all these Black men working together, getting along, and it makes me think that maybe there are a lot of Black men doing this."[12]

These findings are amplified in later research by Bartanen and Grissom showing that Black principals are more likely than White principals to hire and retain Black teachers, a factor known to improve Black students' academic outcomes.[13] The evidence suggests that principals are hiring Black teachers because they are seeking a modeling effect and desiring to build a school culture that reflects Black cultural norms. Related to principals' recruitment and retention of Black teachers is the fact that Black teachers are more likely than Whites to remain in a school when its population of Black students and students living in poverty increases. Black teachers in training also are more likely than their White peers to express a desire to serve in Black and high-poverty schools.

Notably, Bartanen and Grissom found "positive effects of Black principals on Black student math achievement after the principal's first year."[14] Other studies have shown that because of shared racial/ethnic and cultural experiences, Black and other principals of color can strengthen school ties with Black communities and ensure that their schools' instructional practices and policies reflect Black history and cultural achievements and that disciplinary policies do not unduly penalize and marginalize Black students.

HOW CHILDREN AND YOUTH INTERPRET LACK OF TEACHER DIVERSITY

Diversifying the nation's teaching force is essential to the racial and ethnic integration of American society, a goal that most Americans say they support. Numerous quantitative and qualitative studies show that Black principals and teachers make a positive difference, spurring academic achievement and attainment and improving social outcomes for Black students. Furthermore, given their superior academic credentials, pedagogical expertise, and caring attitudes, Black educators positively impact all students. There is clear evidence that the presence of Black educators also dispels myths of racial inferiority and incompetence.[15]

After *Brown*, the loss of Black principals and teachers was keenly felt by Black students, who often found themselves in unwelcoming and hostile new surroundings. Their intellectual models, guides, protectors, and encouragers were gone. The ones who would model and teach them how to negotiate a racist world were gone, as was any evidence of Black history, intellectual, or cultural accomplishments in the school's curriculum and culture. In many ways, Black students were desegregated into school deserts with no oases.

These students knew then what they know now: too many schools are not built for them. This knowledge constitutes a silent suffering in young minds that can stymie formation of a positive identity, hinder cultivation of a love of learning, and grow a cynicism about the "game of schooling."

When Black and White students see nothing (or very little) in the school environment that speaks of Black history, cultural contributions, and excellence, it is debilitating to the psychological development of both. In this void and without interception, the Black child is susceptible to an ignorance about Black culture that can breed feelings of racial inferiority, isolation, an acceptance of White as normative, and belief in Black exceptionalism. In this void and without disruption, the White child is susceptible to the pathological myth of White superiority and the utter and debased ignorance (and sometimes violence) it inspires.

Prior to *Brown*, 35 percent to 50 percent of teachers and an equivalent percentage of principals were Black. Today, there is no state that even begins to approach these percentages.[16] Yet it is indisputable that all children benefit from experiencing a diverse school staff, because this diversity teaches all children in a vibrant, multicultural America the vital lessons that models of intellectual authority and leadership are not exclusively White—nor should they be. The work of generating knowledge, expressing creativity, solving the world's problems, and leading into a new future belongs to all people and can best be achieved by the diverse people of our nation and the world, all working together.

INVENTING TEACHER SHORTAGES, ALTERNATIVE CERTIFICATION, AND SCHOOL REFORM MODELS

The mass closure of Black schools and influx of Black students into previously all-White schools led to an increased need for principals and teachers in desegregating schools. But with Black principals and teachers illegally pushed out of school systems, White superintendents and school boards found themselves in a quandary: Who was going to lead the schools and teach the swelling numbers of students? Pressed by the need to hire more educators, they manufactured principal and teacher shortages, turning almost exclusively to Whites outside the profession, vacating state requirements for education degrees and teacher licensure, and creating fast tracks into the classroom through emergency certification. The NAACP and NASSP reported as late as 1971 that Black principals and teachers who held certification and years of experience were being replaced by White principals and teachers who had no certification, no experience in the communities in which they were placed, and, in the case of White teachers, were often teaching in areas in which they were not fully certified.

Given these realities, it is unlikely that the generations of Black principals and teachers who were illegally fired, demoted, and dismissed would support modern-day fast-track alternative certification programs that place noncertified individuals as teachers, primarily in schools serving Black and poor students. These deposed Black educators would likely also distrust contemporary school "reform" models such as vouchers, school choice, and charter schools. After all, these were among the very mechanisms that they experienced during the decades-long stalling of *Brown*'s progress that siphoned public tax dollars from desegregating public schools and annihilated their careers as principals and teachers. Furthermore, it is worth noting that these various "reform" mechanisms may never have come into existence had a generation of uniquely qualified Black educators—people with superior academic credentials, professional licensure, an attitudinal commitment to democratic ideals, consistent activism against the ideology of racism, and experience with integrated society—been integrated into the public school system rather than expelled from it.

What does it mean to American public schooling, the quest for integrated schools, the formulation of progressive and inclusive education and social policies, Black children's academic achievement and attainment, and the erosion of racism to have lost these professionals—a nationwide cadre of exceptionally trained educators who would never be replaced?

Had these generations of Black principals and teachers (who against all odds attained their own education achievements and successfully taught Black students) been integrated into schools after *Brown*, how might the nation, its schools, and its citizenry have benefited? Against every challenge and even terror, these Black educators led generations out of illiteracy, modeled civic engagement, and offered hope and a future. What could these remarkable professionals and citizens have done with America's schools if they had not been thwarted and deterred at every turn? It is difficult to untangle the damage done from any progress made. What is sure: this is the legacy our public schools and our nation's children live with and must overcome.

EPILOGUE

DESEGREGATION OF THE nation's principal and teacher workforce is "a goal that we have recognized to be an important aspect of the basic task of achieving a school system wholly free from racial discrimination" proclaimed the *Bradley v. School Board* decision in 1965. More than half a century later, the nation has not yet achieved this basic task. In fact, failed desegregation and racism continue to negatively shape Black students' school experiences.

Notably, Black and poor students are 70 percent more likely to have teachers who are not certified or do not have college majors or minors in the subject area they teach. This pattern prevails across four subject areas: math, science, social studies, and English. At the same time, 84 percent of Black students (compared with 66 percent of White students) attend schools in high-stakes test states, where passing a state-mandated standardized test means the difference between grade promotion, retention, and high school graduation.

How is it that the bar is raised on what students are expected to know, but lowered on who stands before them to teach? Compounding these classroom effects are other factors that systematically and consistently limit Black and poor students' opportunities to learn. These students languish in schools that are underfunded, lack contemporary technology, offer fewer gifted and AP courses and a curriculum more focused on standardized tests, and have short-tenured superintendents, a revolving door of principals, and high turnover rates among teachers.

About 7 percent, or 266,000 of the nation's 3.8 million public school teachers, are Black. About 7.5 million public school students are Black; this number represents 15 percent of all the nation's 50 million public school students. Certainly, simply increasing the number of Black principals and teachers will not solve all that challenges of public education; nor should Black educators be the only educators responsible for reaching and teaching Black students. Research does suggest, however, that increasing contact with Black principals and teachers will increase Black students' academic achievement and educational attainment. Also, given their generally superior academic credentials and professional experiences, having Black principals and superintendents influence and shape school and district instructional policies and funding could also help.

Why are we still struggling to mark real progress in education? Since the arrival of Black students in previously all-White schools after *Brown*, education policies and practices have been informed almost exclusively by White social scientists, psychometricians, educational leaders, local elected officials, philanthropists, and their acolytes. These individuals have no deep-tissue knowledge about Black communities and history. Without this foundational knowledge and in the face of pervasive negative social commentary about Blacks, White powerbrokers believed and actively reproduced deficit perspectives about Blacks. Their erroneous perspectives made (and continue to make) their way into policies; federal, state, and philanthropic funding streams; and intervention programs. Rarely have any of these mechanisms taken aim at root causes of disparities. So the disparities remain. And when the disparities remain, Black and other communities of color are viewed as "beyond intervention."

The recommendations that follow are intended to help remedy the long-term harm done to the nation's public education system and its students caused by the displacement of Black educational leaders after *Brown*. The harm is not just the decimation of Black principals and teachers and the subsequent underrepresentation of Blacks in the nation's educator workforce. The harm is what was amplified with the loss of Black educators, including a phalanx of racist theories, psychometric tools, and education policies and practices that asserted Black intellectual and cultural inferiority (overtly and subtly) and worked to constrict Blacks' educational opportunity and achievement.

RECOMMENDATIONS

The question is, what can be done at this point? Following are nine concrete suggestions that could make a positive difference in today's public schools:

- **Tell the history and refute the myth.** The history detailed in *Jim Crow's Pink Slip* refutes the national myth that after *Brown*, Blacks fled principalships and teaching positions to pursue new career options not previously open to them. This presumption is untrue. The historical record shows that after *Brown* in the dual-system states, exceptionally credentialed and effective Black principals and teachers were purposely purged from public schools and replaced by less-qualified Whites. This disturbing history needs to frame policy and practice discussions about educator workforce diversity, because many of the levers that were used to eliminate Black principal and teacher leadership after *Brown* are still in use today. As Epstein asserts in the *Whitening of the American Teaching Force*, "Understanding that the composition of the teaching force is a case of institutional racism, rather than a problem of recruitment, is critical to formulating an effective response."[1]
- **Interrogate teacher licensure entrance examinations and cut scores.** After *Brown*, dual-system states worked with the Education Testing Service (ETS) to create new teacher licensure examinations with the explicit purpose of states using the exams and cut-off scores to eliminate Black teacher prospects. (Even Black educators who held licensure prior to *Brown* were subject to the newly created exams). A nearly sixty-year battle to create and enforce equitable entrance requirements to the teaching profession has led some researchers to assert that the "various standardized test requirements [entrance and licensure examinations] essentially operate as a job reservation and segregation system for Whites."[2] Others have concluded that continuing the teacher testing regime will not help the nation meet the teacher diversity goals it espouses and that organized resistance is a necessary strategy in order to advance teacher diversity. As Epstein writes,

  > Recruiting individual nonwhites to jump over the hurdles of the credentialing process cannot provide enough teachers to end the

> massive urban schoolteacher shortage (Cartledge, 1995). We need organized resistance to the exclusionary credential laws. An effective national campaign would require a coalition of civil rights and education organizations to oppose credentialing regulations that disproportionately exclude nonwhite college graduates and to insist that such measures be countered institutionally to mitigate their impact.[3]

Licensure examination pass rate disparities between Black and White teacher candidates exist today in every state using such tests. These tests effectively qualify nearly all White teacher candidates and disqualify the majority of Black teacher candidates. Yet licensure examinations continue to be used as a screen for entrance into the profession. Given the history of *why* entrance licensure examinations were created and *how* they have been used, states should be incentivized to interrogate how teacher licensure examination cut scores are set, develop remedying strategies that reduce the negative impact entrance licensure exam cut scores have on Black and Hispanic/Latinx teacher candidates, and evolve measures of professional competence that do not maintain racial/ethnic disparities for entrance into the teaching profession.

- **Examine how the transfer of Black principal and teacher jobs to Whites affected/affects the Black-White wealth gap.** After *Brown*, the illegal handover of nearly 100,000 jobs held by Black principals and teachers to lesser-qualified Whites constituted a wealth transfer. The case for reparations needs to include an accounting of the financial devastation the illegal firings, dismissals, demotions, and other economic reprisals created in Black communities, versus the concomitant economic gains by Whites.
- **Invest in the preparation, recruitment, and retention of a new generation of educator preparation program faculty at colleges and universities.** The majority of Blacks who earn doctoral degrees do so in education and the social sciences. Yet Black academics remain underrepresented on tenured faculties in the nation's schools and colleges of education, except at HBCUs. Beginning in the 2017–2018 academic year and for the first time in US public colleges, students of color constituted a majority of undergraduate students in public colleges and universities. However, the likelihood of Black and other

college students of color having Black and other faculty of color teach them is slim. In fact, Black faculty constitute only about 6 percent of higher education faculty overall (although this percentage is considerably higher at HBCUs, where Black faculty predominate). In many ways, the case for diversifying higher education faculty mirrors that for public school faculty. There is evidence to suggest that diversifying the ranks of higher education faculty can positively affect the recruitment and retention, as well as the professional aspirations, of Black and other college students of color. In order to reach the nation's educator workforce diversity goals, schools and colleges of education will increasingly need to model the recruitment, retention, and promotion of Black and other underrepresented faculty of color in their own ranks.

- **Invest in HBCU teacher preparation programs.** Though HBCUs constitute less than 4 percent of the nation's colleges/universities, they prepare 50 percent of the nation's Black teachers. Prioritizing these institutions with federal and state funding can assist with widening the Black teacher pipeline.
- **Invest in Hispanic-serving institutions (HSIs) teacher preparation programs.** HSIs graduate 90 percent of the nation's Hispanic/Latinx teachers. Prioritizing these institutions with federal and state funding can assist in widening the Hispanic/Latinx teacher pipeline. There is also a significant Afro-Latinx student population attending HSIs. If recruited into teacher education, these prospective teachers could bridge multiple racial/ethnic, cultural, and linguistic barriers.
- **Invest in the preparation of Black superintendents.** Invest in and recruit superintendents who have expertise in and a track record of achieving academic progress with Black and other students of color. These leaders' philosophical dedication to public education should also be evidenced by their commitment to lay leadership of school districts (that is, maintenance of school board governance); a refusal to close schools in poor, Black communities in exchange for proliferating charter schools managed by for-profit entities; and an ability to interrupt corporate models of schools reform such as vouchers, for-profit charter school networks, and disproportionate placement of alternatively certified teachers as the teachers of record in schools serving students of color from families experiencing poverty.

Notably, all these approaches are apparatuses with origins in White resistance to *Brown* and have been shown to exacerbate educational inequities.

- **Invest in anti-racist curriculums and high school ethnic studies models.** These curriculum interventions have been shown to improve student engagement, critical thinking skills, and high school graduation rates for racial/ethnic minority students.
- **Diversify curriculum materials, instructional models, professional development, and textbooks.** Through their imagery and content, such thoughtfully designed educational materials will centrally—not peripherally—address the academic interests and needs of Black and all other students.

CONCLUSION

The economic well-being of the nation's citizens and the vibrancy of its schools must be inspired by our collective will to eradicate the isolation and ills of racism and poverty. Historically, these ills have been tied to educational opportunity and quality—each of which was severely compromised with the decimation of black educators after *Brown*.

At root, much of the discussion in *Jim Crow's Pink Slip* is about whose children we believe are worthy of investment and whose are subject to disinvestment. If our nation's leaders and citizens desire to undo the missed opportunity that the generations of purged Black principals and teachers represented for creating truly integrated schools, a new commitment will emerge. It will be a commitment to dismember the infrastructure, mechanisms, and policies that have us ideologically and financially disinvesting from children of color and children from families experiencing poverty. It will be a determination to reformulate state, district, and school-based policies and practices that routinely privilege White and affluent students at the (literal) expense of students of color and students living in poverty. It will be a dogged insistence that we move past a deficit perspective about Black and other students of color and create teaching and learning environments that affirm the intellectual capacity and cultural heritage of all students. It will reflect an abiding belief and dedicated adherence to democratic principles as the path to revolutionary change.

Children are watching and learning from us. The Black, Brown, and poor children who are languishing in too many underfunded and inadequate schools will soon be the majority of Americans. They already constitute the majority of public school students.

What will it mean for American democracy when these young people—many of whom have been pushed and held at the margins of the social, political, and economic order—are the majority? Will their commitment to democracy and public schooling be resonant, or will it be absent?

GLOSSARY

THE FOLLOWING terms and abbreviations are used extensively in *Jim Crow's Pink Slip*. This glossary provides definitions for items that may be less familiar to some readers.

AFT American Federation of Teachers, a professional association and teachers union founded in 1916.

ATA American Teachers Association, a professional association and teachers union representing Black educators during the era of legal segregation. Predecessors include the National Colored Teachers Association (1906–1907) and the National Association of Teachers in Colored Schools (1907–1937). ATA merged with the National Education Association (NEA) in 1966.

Brown I* and *Brown II (Brown v. Topeka, Kansas, Board of Education) On May 17, 1954, the US Supreme Court unanimously declared that "in the field of public education the doctrine of 'separate but equal' has no place." In declaring that "separate educational facilities are inherently unequal," the court explicitly overturned the reasoning of *Plessy v. Ferguson*.

Brown II, issued in 1955, decreed that the dismantling of separate school systems for Black and White students could proceed with "all deliberate speed," a phrase that pleased neither supporters nor opponents of integration. Unintentionally, it opened the way for various strategies of resistance to the decision.[1]

Jim Crow The Jim Crow Museum of Racist Memorabilia at Ferris State University (Grand Rapids, Michigan) offers this descriptive and historical definition:

> Jim Crow was the name of the racial caste system which operated primarily, but not exclusively, in southern and border states between 1877 and the mid-1960s. Jim Crow was more than a series of rigid anti-black laws. It was a way of life.
>
> Under Jim Crow, African Americans were relegated to the status of second-class citizens. Jim Crow represented the legitimization of anti-black racism. Many Christian ministers and theologians taught that whites were the Chosen people, blacks were cursed to be servants, and God supported racial segregation. Craniologists, eugenicists, phrenologists, and Social Darwinists, at every educational level, buttressed the belief that blacks were innately intellectually and culturally inferior to whites. Pro-segregation politicians gave eloquent speeches on the great danger of integration: the mongrelization of the white race. Newspaper and magazine writers routinely referred to blacks as niggers, coons, and darkies; and worse, their articles reinforced anti-black stereotypes. Even children's games portrayed blacks as inferior beings (see "From Hostility to Reverence: 100 Years of African-American Imagery in Games"). All major societal institutions reflected and supported the oppression of blacks.
>
> The Jim Crow system was undergirded by the following beliefs or rationalizations: whites were superior to blacks in all important ways, including but not limited to intelligence, morality, and civilized behavior; sexual relations between blacks and whites would produce a mongrel race which would destroy America; treating blacks as equals would encourage interracial sexual unions; any activity which suggested social equality encouraged interracial sexual relations; if necessary, violence must be used to keep blacks at the bottom of the racial hierarchy.[2]

NAACP The National Association for the Advancement of Colored People.

NABSE The National Alliance of Black School Educators.

NASSP The National Association of Secondary School Principals.

NEA The National Education Association. Founded in 1857 as the National Teachers Association (NTA), the organization merged with the American Teachers Association (the Black teachers organization) in 1966.

Pink slip A notice of dismissal from employment.

NOTES

PREFACE

1. The history told here is unique to African Americans and not other Black people from throughout the diaspora (African, Carribbean, etc.) who are now in America. Thus, for the purposes of this book, "Black" and "African American" are used interchangeably.

2. W. E. B. Du Bois, "A Negro Schoolmaster in the South," *The Atlantic* (January 1899), https://www.theatlantic.com/magazine/archive/1899/01/a-negro-school master-in-the-south/400028/.

3. W. E. B. Du Bois, "A Negro Schoolmaster in the South." 28.

4. Richard Powell, *Black Art: A Cultural History* (London: Thames & Hudson, 1977), 24–25.

5. Rachel Berenson Perry, "The Paintings of William Edouard Scott," *American Art Review*, March–April 2007, 82.

6. James D. Anderson, *The Education of Blacks in the South, 1860–1935* (Chapel Hill: The University of North Carolina Press, 1988).

7. Vanessa Siddle Walker and Ulysses Byas, *Hello Professor: A Black Principal and Professional Leadership in a Segregated Community* (Chapel Hill: The University of North Carolina Press, 2009), 1.

8. Most notably, these include Walker and Byas, *Hello Professor*; David S. Cecelski, *Along Freedom Road: Hyde County, North Carolina, and the Fate of Black Schools in the South* (Chapel Hill: The University of North Carolina Press, 1994); Adam Fairclough, *A Class of Their Own: Black Teachers in the Segregated South* (Cambridge, MA: Harvard University Press, 2007); Carol F. Karpinski, "Bearing the Burden of Desegregation: Black Principals and *Brown*," *Urban Education* 41, no. 3 (2006): 237–276; Michael Fultz, "The Displacement of Black Educators Post-*Brown*: An Overview and Analysis," *History of Education Quarterly* 44, no. 1 (2004): 11–45, doi:10.1111/j.1748-5959.2004.tb00144.x; and Linda Tillman,

"African American Principals and the Legacy of *Brown*," *Review of Research in Education* 28 (2004): 101–146.

9. Fairclough, *A Class of Their Own*, 390.

10. Tillman, "African American Principals and the Legacy of *Brown*, 101–146.

11. Kathleen A. Welsch, "History as Complex Storytelling," *College Composition and Communication* 50, no. 1(1998): 116–122.

12. Welsch, "History as Complex Storytelling."

13. Henry Wiencek, *Master of the Mountain: Thomas Jefferson and His Slaves* (New York: Farrar, Straus and Giroux, 2012).

14. Chris Lorenz, "Drawing the Line: 'Scientific' History Between Myth-Making and Myth-Breaking," in *Narrating the Nation: Representations in History, Media and the Arts*, ed. Stefan Berger, Linas Eriksonas, and Andrew Mycock (New York and Oxford: Berghahn, 2008), 35–55. http://culturahistorica.org/wp-content/uploads/2020/02/2lorenz-drawing_the_line.pdf.

15. Karpinski, "Bearing the Burden"; Fairclough, *A Class of Their Own.*

16. Karpinski, "Bearing the Burden."

17. Frank Manheim, "Before Desegregation, Black Kansas City High Schools Dominated in Science Awards," *Kansas City Star*, May 28, 2021.

18. E. D. Taylor, *The Original Black Elite: Daniel Murray and the Story of a Forgotten Era* (New York: HarperCollins, 2017), 6.

CHAPTER 1

1. National Center for Educational Statistics, 2020.

2. Linda Tillman, "African American Principals and the Legacy of *Brown*" *Review of Research in Education* 28 (2004): 101–46.

3. Leslie Fenwick, "Why We Should Diversify the Overwhelmingly White US Teaching Force and How," *Washington Post*, May 21, 2015.

4. Leon Panetta, interview by the author, March 29, 2019.

5. *Hearings before the Select Committee on Equal Educational Opportunity of the United States Senate, Part 10—Displacement and Present Status of Black School Principals in Desegregated School Districts*, 92nd Cong. (1971) (Statement of Senator Edward W. Brooke, R-MA), 4903.

6. Letter to Darla Buchanan, *Brown v. Board of Education of Topeka*, 1954.

7. Lumen Learning, https://courses.lumenlearning.com/ushistory2ay/chapter/the-new-south-and-the-problem-of-race-2/.

8. Joseph P. Reidy, *Illusions of Emancipation: The Pursuit of Freedom and Equality in the Twilight of Slavery* (Chapel Hill: University of North Carolina Press, 2019), 338.

9. Reidy, *Illusions of Emancipation*, 339.

10. John A. Kirk, "Not Quite Black and White: School Desegregation in Arkansas, 1954–1966," *The Arkansas Historical Quarterly* 70, no. 3 (2011), 225–57.

11. Hearings before Senate Select Committee on EEO, Part 10 (1971), 4904.

12. Hearings, 4914.

13. Hearings, 5321.

14. Hearings, 5082.

15. Roy Wilkins, "The Role of the National Association for the Advancement of Colored People in the Desegregation Process," *Social Problems* 2, no. 4 (1955), 202.

16. Wilkins, "The Role of the National Association for the Advancement of Colored People," 203.

17. Hearings before Senate Select Committee on EEO, Part 10 (1971), 4961.

18. Hearings, 4914.

19. Hearings, 4907.

20. Hearings, 4908.

21. Hearings, 4907.

22. Hearings, 4969.

23. Hearings, testimony of Dr. Bettie M. Smith, 4922.

24. Hearings, 4921–22.

25. Robert W. Hooker, *Displacement of Black Teachers in the Eleven Southern States* (Nashville, TN: Race Relations Information Center, 1970), 3; reprinted in Hearings before Senate Select Committee on EEO, Part 10 (1971) (Appendix 5), 5341–89.

26. Hooker, *Displacement*, 5

27. Hearings before Senate Select Committee on EEO, Part 10 (1971), 5185.

28. Brief *Amicus curiae* for the National Education Association, US Court of Appeals for the Fifth Circuit, No. 30,338 (1971), 5; reprinted in Hearings before Senate Select Committee on EEO, Part 10 (1971) (Appendix 4: 5025–5119), 5038.

29. Brief *Amicus curiae* for NEA, 10–14; Hearings, 5043–47.

30. Hearings before Senate Select Committee on EEO, Part 10 (1971) (extracts from Dr. Albert Baxter's dissertation), 5180.

31. Hearings, 5188.

32. Hearings, 4952.

33. Hearings, 5084.

34. Hearings, 5036.

35. Hearings, 5084.

36. Hearings, 5084.

37. NAACP Legal Defense and Education Fund, Inc., "Program to Protect Negro Teachers from Dismissal as a Result of the Integration of Public Schools," memorandum (n.d.), 2.

38. NAACP LDF, "Program to Protect Negro Teachers, 2.

39. Hearings before Senate Select Committee on EEO, Part 10 (1971), 5338.

40. Hearings, 4908.

41. Hooker, *Displacement*, 26.

42. Hooker, 23.

43. Vanessa Siddle Walker, "African American Teachers in Segregated Schools in the South, 1940–1969," *American Educational Research Journal* 38, no. 4 (2001): 751–79.

44. Hooker, *Displacement*, 6.

45. Hearings before Senate Select Committee of EEO, Part 10 (1971) (Appendix 5: Georgia Teachers & Education Association), 5189.

46. Hearings before Senate Select Committee of EEO, Part 10 (1971) (Appendix 5: Desegregation and the Rights of Educators in Louisiana), 5196–13.

47. Hooker, *Displacement*, 37.

48. Brief *Amicus curiae* for NEA, 60; Hearings, 5093.

49. Hearings before Senate Select Committee of EEO, Part 10 (1971), (Appendix 5: Analysis of Problems by States: Texas), 5389.

50. Hooker, *Displacement*, 34–35.

51. Hooker, 35–6.

52. Hooker, 7.

53. Hooker, 23.

54. Hooker, 19, 27, 21, 38, 22.

55. "Government Ponders Plan to Help Black Teachers in Desegregated Schools," *Jet*, June 1, 1972, 24.

56. Hooker, *Displacement*, 14.

57. Hearings before Senate Select Committee of EEO, Part 10 (1971), 5381.

58. Hearings, 4956.

59. National Center for Education Statistics, 2013–14.

60. Hooker, *Displacement*, 13

61. Hooker, 13.

62. Hearings before Senate Select Committee of EEO, Part 10 (1971), 5188–5189.

63. Hearings, 5122.

64. Hearings, 5375.

65. Michael Fultz, "The Displacement of Black Educators Post-*Brown*: An Overview and Analysis," *History of Education Quarterly* 44, no. 1 (2004), 26.

66. Hearings before Senate Select Committee of EEO, Part 10 (1971), 5356.

67. Hearings, 5382.

68. Hearings, 5180.

69. Hearings, 5361.

70. Hearings, 5181.

71. Kirk, "Not Quite Black and White."

CHAPTER 2

1. Revised Statutes of Missouri, Section 9622, 1929.

2. Reid E. Jackson, "Financial Aid Given by Southern States to Negroes for Out-of-State Study," *The Journal of Negro Education* 13, no. 1 (1944): 30–39.

3. Jackson, "Financial Aid."

4. Maryland Session Laws, 1937, p. 1071.

5. Annotated Code of Maryland, 506.

6. Texas House Bill No. 255, "Appropriations for Institutions of Higher Learning," 359.

7. Jackson, "Financial Aid."

8. Jackson.

9. Jackson.

10. Jacqueline Jordan Irvine and Leslie T. Fenwick, "Teachers and Teaching for the New Millennium: The Role of HBCUs," *Journal of Negro Education* 80, no. 3 (2011): 197–208.

11. *Hearings before the Select Committee on Equal Educational Opportunity of the United States Senate, Part 10—Displacement and Present Status of Black School Principals in Desegregated School Districts*, 92nd Cong. (1971) (Testimony of Dr. Bettie M. Smith), 4921.

12. Hearings, 4981.

13. Hearings, 4980.

14. Robert W. Hooker, *Displacement of Black Teachers in the Eleven Southern States* (Nashville, TN: Race Relations Information Center, 1970), 14; reprinted in Hearings (Appendix 5): 5341–89.

15. Hearings before Senate Select Committee on EEO, Part 10 (1971), 5281–5284.

16. Hearings, 5388.

17. Hearings, 5325.

18. Hearings, 5287.

19. Hearings, 5384.

20. Hearings, 5499–5000.

21. Al-Tony Gilmore, *All the People: NEA's Legacy of Inclusion and Its Minority Presidents.* (Washington, DC: NEA), 2008.

22. Hearings before the Senate Select Committee on EEO, Part 10 (1971), 4950–51.

23. Hearings, 4965.

24. Hearings, 5340.

25. Hearings, 4943.

26. Hearings, 4959.

27. Hearings, 5348.

28. Hearings, 4945.

29. Hearings, 5390.

30. Hearings, 4908, 4905.

31. Hearings, 4904.

32. Hearings, 5000.

33. Hearings, 5084–85.

34. Hearings, 4967.

35. Hearings, 4915.

36. Hearings, 5331.

37. Hearings, 4941.

38. Thurgood Marshall, *Report on the Department of Teacher Information and Security, January 1 to June 30, 1955*, 2.

39. Hearings before the Senate Select Committee on EEO, Part 10 (1971), 5188.

40. Hearings, 4915.

41. Hearings, 4936.

42. Hearings, 4966.

43. Lavon W. Bracey and Arthur L. Dawson, *A Brave Little Cookie* (Windemere, FL: Lavon Business Services, Inc., 2019), 18–27.

44. Bracey and Dawson, *A Brave Little Cookie*, 18–27.

45. Hearings before the Senate Select Committee on EEO, Part 10 (1971), 4966.

46. Hearings, 4966.

47. Hearings, 4966.

48. Hearings, statement of John Oliver Killens, 5268.

49. Hearings, 5085.

50. Hearings, 4987.

51. Hearings, 5188.

51. Michael Fultz, "The Displacement of Black Educators Post-Brown: An Overview and Analysis," *History of Education Quarterly* 44, no. 1 (2004), 37.

53. Hearings before the Senate Select Committee on EEO, Part 10 (1971), 4914.

54. Hearings, 5084.

55. Hearings, 5339.

56. Hearings, 4956–57.

57. Hearings, 4984–85.

58. Vanessa Siddle Walker, "Valued Segregated Schools for African American Children in the South, 1935–1969: A Review of Common Themes and Characteristics," *Review of Educational Research* 70, no. 3 (2000), 253–85.

59. David S. Cecelski, *Along Freedom Road: Hyde County, North Carolina, and the Fate of Black Schools in the South* (Chapel Hill: University of North Carolina Press, 1994), 63.

60. Cecelski, *Along Freedom Road*, 62–63.

61. Walker, "Valued Segregated Schools."

62. Linda C. Tillman, ed. "Pushing Back Resistance: African American Discourses on School Leadership" (special issue), *Educational Administration Quarterly* 41, no. 4 (2005), 175.

63. Hearings before Senate Select Committee on EEO, Part 10 (1971), 4985.

64. Hearings, 5387.

65. Hearings, 5387.

66. Hearings, 5000.

67. Hearings, 4947.

68. Hearings, 4985.

CHAPTER 3

1. *Hearings before the Select Committee on Equal Educational Opportunity of the United States Senate, Part 10—Displacement and Present Status of Black School Principals in Desegregated School Districts*, 92nd Cong. (1971), 4997.

2. Hearings, 4996.

3. Hearings, 4996.

4. Hearings, 4995.

5. Hearings, 5345.

6. Hearings, 5187.

7. Hearings, 4919.

8. Hearings, 4984.

9. Hearings, 5385.

10. Hearings, 4943.

11. Hearings, 4981.

12. Hearings, 4943.

13. Hearings, 5385.

14. Hearings, 4999.

15. Hearings, 4993.

16. Hearings, 4993.

17. Hearings, 4993–94.

18. Hearings, 5386.

19. Hearings, 5336.

20. Hearings, 4965.

21. Hearings, 4984.

22. Hearings, 4954.

23. Lee v. Macon County, 5 Cir. 1971, 448 F.2d 746; Bivins v. Bibb County, 5 Cir. 1972, 460 F.2d 430 [1972]; Bell et al. v. West Point Municipal School District, 5 Cir. 1971, 446 F.2d 1362; Gordon v. Jefferson Davis Parish, 5 Cir. 1971, 446 F.2d 266; Wright v. Board of Public Instruction of Alachua County, 5 Cir. 1970, 431 F.2d 1200; Carr v. Montgomery County, 5 Cir. 1970, 429 F.2d 382; Choctaw County Board of Education v. United States, 5 Cir. 1969, 417 F.2d 845.

24. Felder v. Harnett County Board of Education, 409 F.2d 1070 (4th Cir. 1969).

25. Hearings before Senate Select Committee on EEO, Part 10 (1971), 4985.

26. Hearings, 4972.

27. Hearings, 4984.

28. Hearings, 5332.

29. American Friends Service Committee Report, 1970, 52–57.

30. AFSC Report, 54, 55.

31. Hearings, 5184.

32. Hearings, 5184.

33. David S. Cecelski, *Along Freedom Road: Hyde County North Carolina, and the Fate of Black Schools in the South* (Chapel Hill: The University of North Carolina Press, 1994), 27.

34. James D. Anderson, *The Education of Blacks in the South, 1860–1935* (Chapel Hill: The University of North Carolina Press, 1988), 149.

35. Diane Granat, *Saving the Rosenwald Schools: Preserving African American History*, http://www.aliciapatterson.org/APF2004/Granat/Granat.html. Granat received a fellowship from the Alicia Patterson Foundation to research *Julius Rosenwald: America's Forgotten Philanthropist*, in 2002.

36. Anderson, *Education of Blacks in the South*, 153.

37. Granat, *Saving the Rosenwald Schools.*

38. Anderson, *Education of Blacks in the South*, 166.

39. Tom Hanchett, "Saving the South's Rosenwald Schools," *History South*, 2004, http://www.rosenwaldplans.org/history.html.

40. Granat, *Saving the Rosenwald Schools.*

41. Cecelski, *Along Freedom Road*, 59.

42. Cecelski, 80.

43. Vanessa Siddle Walker, *Their Highest Potential: An African American School Community in the Segregated South* (Chapel Hill, NC: University of North Carolina Press, 1996), 254.

44. Mary Gibson Hundley, *The Dunbar Story, 1870–1955* (New York: Vantage Press, 1965).

45. Hundley, *The Dunbar Story*, 45.

46. Wilma Bonner et al., *The Sumner Story: Capturing Our History, Preserving Our Legacy* (New York: Morgan James Publishing, 2011).

47. Anderson, *Education of Blacks in the South*, 198.

48. Anderson, 199.

49. Bonner et al., *The Sumner Story*; Walker, *Their Highest Potential*; Cecelski, *Along Freedom Road.*

50. Cecelski, *Along Freedom Road*, 65.

51. Walker, *Their Highest Potential.*

52. Michele Foster, *Black Teachers on Teaching* (New York: New Press, 1997), 5.

53. Anderson, *Education of Blacks in the South*,190.

54. Hearings before Senate Select Committee on EEO, Part 10 (1971), 4984.

55. Anderson, *Education of Blacks in the South*, 285.

CHAPTER 4

1. Others in the Oval Office at the time included Chief of Staff H. R. Halderman, Secretary of State Henry Kissinger, Counsel and Assistant for Domestic Affairs John Ehrlichman, and White House lawyer Edward L. Morgan.

2. *Hearings before the Select Committee on Equal Educational Opportunity of the United States Senate, Part 10—Displacement and Present Status of Black School Principals in Desegregated School Districts*, 92nd Cong. (1971), 4950–4951.

3. Hearings, 4948.

4. Hearings, 4948–49.

5. Hearings, 4949.

6. Hearings, 4950–51.

7. Hearings, 4951.

8. Hearings, 4951.

9. J. H. Wilkerson III, "The Supreme Court and Southern School Desegregation, 1955–1970: A Historical Analysis," *Virginia Law Review* 64, no. 4 (1978): 485–559, 542.

10. Wilkerson, "The Supreme Court and Southern School Desegregation," 545.

11. Wilkerson, 545.

12. Wilkerson, 543, 547.

13. William Jefferson, "School Desegregation and the Black Teacher: A Search for Effective Remedies," *Tulane Law Review* 55, no. 8 (1973), 55–84.

14. Hearings before Senate Select Committee on EEO, Part 10 (1971), 4951.

15. Hearings, 5087.

16. Hearings, 5086, 5116.

17. Hearings, 5087, 5108.

18. Hearings, 5102.

19. Hearings, 5116.

20. Hearings, 5094.

21. Jefferson, "School Desegregation and the Black Teacher," 77.

22. Hearings, 5076.

23. Lee v. Macon County Board of Education, Muscle Shoals School System, 5 Cir., 1971, 453 F.2d 1104, p. 7.

24. Lee v. Macon County Board of Education, 5.

25. Lee v. Macon County Board of Education, 8.

26. Reynolds v. Abbeville County School District, 554 F2d 638, 4th Circuit, 1977, p. 2.

27. Reynolds v. Abbeville County School District, 3.

28. Reynolds v. Abbeville County School District, 8.

29. Carol F. Karpinski, "Bearing the Burden of Desegregation: Black Principals and *Brown*." *Urban Education* 41, no. 3 (2006): 237–276.

30. Hearings, *998*.

31. Karpinski, "Bearing the Burden."

32. http://www.presidency.ucsb.edu/ws/print.pht?pid=2923.

33. The Guide, HEW "Program for Displaced Students and Educators" (Washington, DC: Office of Education, 1972), 3.

34. The Guide, 4.

35. American Friends Service Committee, *The Status of School Desegregation in the South* (Washington, DC: American Friends Service Committee 1970), 76.

36. American Friends Service Committee, *The Status of School Desegregation in the South*, 6

37. AFSC, The Status of School Desegregation, 2

38. AFSC, 100, 19.

39. AFSC, 7.

40. Hearings, 4970.

41. Hearings, 4972.

42. Donn Rogosin, *Invisible Men: Life in Baseball's Negro Leagues* (New York: Atheneum, 1983), 86–87.

43. Rogosin, *Invisible Men*, 87; Ethan Michaeli. *The Defender: How the Legendary Black Newspaper Changed America* (New York: Houghton Mifflin Harcourt, 2016).

44. *Jet Magazine: The Weekly Negro News Magazine*, September 4, 1952, p. 29.

45. "Bias Against School Principals," *Jet*, July 9, 1970, p. 23.

46. "Nixon's Plan to Retrain Fired Teachers Called Outrage," *Jet*, December 31, 1970, p. 22.

47. "Government Ponders Plan to Help Black Teachers in Desegregated Schools," *Jet*, June 1, 1972, p. 22 .

48. "Government Ponders Plan," 24.

49. *Time Magazine*, July 13, 1970, http://content.time.com/time/subscriber/article/0,33009,909450,00.html.

50. "Mississippi White Women Offered $500 Reward to Use Sex as Trap to Rip Off Black Males," *Jet*, May 16, 1971.

51. Maxine Smith, "Battlefront: Memphis' Crisis in Education" *The Crisis*, January 1970, 26–29.

52. "NAACP Urges HEW to Halt Funds for Biased Schools" *The Crisis*, September 1971, 230.

53. "The Dixie School Charade: Blacks are Deceived by Desegregation Pretense," *Ebony Magazine*, August 1971.

54. "The Dixie School Charade."

55. "Annual Progress Report," *Ebony Magazine*, January 1972.

56. "Whatever Happened to School Desegregation?" *Ebony Magazine*, May 1974.

57. Harry Marin, "Why Black Candidates Lose in Mississippi," *The Crisis*, April 1973, 135–139

58. Marin, "Why Black Candidates Lose."

59. Elizabeth Dowling Taylor, *The Original Black Elite: Daniel Murray and the Story of a Forgotten Era* (New York: HarperCollins, 2017), 408.

60. Wendy Marie Laybourn and Gregory S. Parks, "Omega Psi Phi Fraternity and the Fight for Civil Rights," *Wake Forest Journal of Law and Policy* 6, no. 1 (2016) 213–301.

61. Taylor, *The Original Black Elite*, 409.

62. Taylor, 409.

63. Laybourn and Parks, "Omega Psi Phi Fraternity and the Fight for Civil Rights."

64. Gregory S. Parks, "Lifting as We Climb: The American Council on Human Rights and the Quest for Civil Rights." *American University Journal of Gender, Social Policy & the Law* 25, no. 3 (2017), 261.

65. Gregory S. Parks, Rashawn Ray, and Shawna M. Patterson "Complex Civil Rights Organizations: Alpha Kappa Alpha Sorority, an Exemplar," *Alabama Civil Rights & Civil Liberties Law Review* 6, no. 1 (2014): 125.

66. Samuel Collins III, "Galveston's Jessie McGuire Dent Persisted in Securing Equal Pay for Teachers," Online History Programs, Texas Historical Commission, 2017.

67. Hearings before Senate Select Committee on EEO, Part 10 (1971), 4970.

68. Hearings, 4970.

69. Hearings, 4973–74.
70. Hearings, 4973.
71. Hearings, 4967.
72. Jefferson, "School Desegregation and the Black Teacher," 81.
73. Jefferson, 81.
74. NASSP Board of Directors Minutes of Meeting (November 6–7, 1970), 5.
75. NASSP Newsletter, 1970, p. 3.

CHAPTER 5

1. School Desegration Report of the Subcommittee on Civil and Constitutional Rights of the Committee on the Judiciary House of Representatives, Ninety-Seventh Congress, March 1982, p. 5.

2. Mildred Davis Bruce, "The Richmond School Board and the Desegregation of Richmond Public Schools, 1954 to 1971" (PhD dissertation, College of William and Mary, 1988), 56, doi: https://dx.doi.org/doi:10.25774/w4-fp0k-p519.

3. https://rqbing.tripod.com/1919-1992_staff/willett_h.htm.

4. Jesse. O. McKee, *Mississippi, The Magnolia State* (Atlanta: Clairmont Press Inc, 2005).

5. Martin Luther King, Jr., "How Much Had Schools Really Been Desegregated by 1964?" *The Atlantic Monthly*, May 7, 1964.

6. *Hearings before the Select Committee on Equal Educational Opportunity of the United States Senate, Part 10—Displacement and Present Status of Black School Principals in Desegregated School Districts*, 92nd Cong. (1971), 4941–42.

7. Hearings, 4944.
8. Hearings, 4942.
9. Hearings, 4965.
10. Hearings, 4942.
11. Hearings, 4965, 4966.
12. Hearings, 4965.
13. Hearings, 5390.
14. Hearings, 5393.
15. Hearings, 5397.
16. Hearings, 5411.
17. Hearings, 5440.
18. Hearings, 5040.

CHAPTER 6

1. *Hearings before the Select Committee on Equal Educational Opportunity of the United States Senate, Part 10—Displacement and Present Status of Black School Principals in Desegregated School Districts*, 92nd Cong. (1971), 5440, 5253.

2. Paul Ryan, "NEA School Report Slaps 2 States, Cites Desegregation Failures, *Daily Defender*, November 16, 1970, p. 7.

3. Hearings, 5384, 4936.

4. "Teachers: Segregation by Integration," *Time*, June 18, 1965.

5. Hearings before Senate Select Committee on EEO, Part 10 (1971), 5351.

CHAPTER 7

1. Harry F. Walcott, *The Man in the Principal's Office: An Ethnography* (New York: Holt, Reihardt and Winston, 1973).

2. Leslie T. Fenwick and Chike Akua, "African American Male Teachers and the School Leadership Pipeline: Why More of These Best and Brightest Are Not Principals and Superintendents," in *Black Male Teachers: Diversifying the United States' Teacher Workforce,* ed. Chance Lewis and Ivory Toldson (London: Emerald Press, 2013); Jacqueline J. Irvine and Leslie T. Fenwick, "Teachers and Teaching for the New Millennium: The Role of HBCUs." *The Journal of Negro Education* 80, no. 3 (2011): 197–208; Mary Dilworth and A. L. Brown, "Teachers of Color: Quality and Effectiveness One Way or Another," in *Handbook of Research on Teacher Education*, 3rd ed., ed M. Cochran-Smith, S. Feiman-Nemser, and J. McIntyre (Mahwah, NJ: Lawrence Erlbaum, 2007), 424–44; Beatriz C. Clewell, Michael J. Puma, and Shannon A. McKay, "Does It Matter If My Teacher Looks Like Me? The Impact of Teacher Race and Ethnicity on Student Academic Achievement," paper presented before the American Educational Research Association, Montreal, Canada, April 2005; Kristin Klopfenstein, "Beyond Test Scores: The Impact of African American Teacher Role Models on Rigorous Math Taking," *Contemporary Economic Policy* 23, no. 3 (2005): 416–28; Thomas Dee, "Teachers, Race, and Student Achievement in a Randomized Experiment," *Review of Economics and Statistics* 86, no. 1 (2004): 195–210; Leslie T. Fenwick, *Patterns of Excellence: Policy Perspectives on Diversity in Teaching and School Leadership* (Atlanta: Southern Education Foundation, 2001).

3. Jacqueline J. Irvine, *In Search of Wholeness: African American Teachers and Their Culturally Specific Classroom Practices* (New York: Palgrave, 2002).

4. Eric A. Hanushek, "The Trade-Off Between Child Quantity and Quality," *Journal of Political Economy* 100, no. 1 (February 1992): 84–117; Frederick M. Hess and David L. Leal, "Minority Teachers, Minority Students, and College Matriculation," *Policy Studies Journal* 25 (1997): 235–248.

5. Jason Grissom and Christopher Redding, "Discretion and Disproportionality: Explaining the Underrepresentation of High-Achieving Students of Color on Gifted Programs," American Educational Research Association *Open* 2, no. 1 (January–March 2016): 1–25.

6. S. Gershenson et al., "The Long-Run Impacts of Same Race Teachers" (Working Paper 25254, National Bureau of Economic Research, November 2018), 37.

7. Gershenson et al., "The Long-Run Impacts of Same Race Teachers," 37.

8. Gershenson et al., 37.

9. *Sumner Courier*, October 25, 1946, p. 1.

10. Irvine, *In Search of Wholeness.*

11. Melanie Carter and Leslie T. Fenwick, "Keeping a Close Watch: A Cultural Philosophy of School Change," *NASSP Bulletin*, 85, no. 15 (2001): 15–21.

12. Carter and Fenwick, "Keeping a Close Watch."

13. Brendan Bartanen and Jason Grissom, "School Principal Race and the Hiring and Retention of Racially Diverse Teachers" (EdWorkingPaper, Annenberg Institute at Brown University, 2019), 42.

14. Bartanen and Grissom, "School Principal Race," 42.

15. Mary Dilworth et al., *Millennial Teachers of Color* (Cambridge, MA: Harvard Education Press, 2018); Dilworth and Brown. "Teachers of Color."

16. National Center for Education Statistics, 2017–2018.

EPILOGUE

1. Kitty Kelly Epstein, "The Whitening of the American Teaching Force: A Problem of Recruitment or a Problem of Racism?" *Social Justice* 32, no. 3 (2005): 89–102, 97, http://www.jstor.org/stable/29768323.

2. Epstein, "The Whitening of the American Teaching Force," 95.

3. Epstein, 97.

GLOSSARY

1. https://www.virginiahistory.org/collections-and-resources/virginia-history-explorer/civil-rights-movement-virginia/brown-i-and-brown.

2. https://www.ferris.edu/jimcrow/what.htm.

ACKNOWLEDGMENTS

IN SO MANY WAYS, writing a book is a communal effort. As author of *Jim Crow's Pink Slip*, I have benefited from a community of wise advisors, encouragers, and scholarly peers. I am deeply grateful to each member of this community.

I am fortunate and privileged to know exceptional historians and education historians who have produced award-winning books. Their research, writing, and the theoretical frameworks that shape their work have had a profound impact on my thinking and scholarship. Additionally, these scholar-friends provided inspiration, feedback on earlier versions of my manuscript, and affirmation that my book could make a valuable contribution to the research literature and Americans' understanding of our history. For these and a host of other reasons, I thank Drs. Jaqueline and Russell Irvine, Robert J. Reinstein, James D. Anderson, Joseph Harris, Edna Medford, Joseph Reidy, Vanessa Siddle Walker, and Mary Dilworth. Additionally, I am grateful to Dr. Carlos E. Santiago, Massachusetts Commissioner for Higher Education, who thoughtfully interpreted the relevance of *Jim Crow's Pink Slip* to education equity and to state education policy for K–12 schools and colleges/universities.

For submitting to interviews and sharing invaluable insights with me related to the period covered in *Jim Crow's Pink Slip*, I am indebted to The Honorable Leon Panetta (an advocate of desegregation who headed the Office of Civil Rights during the Nixon Administration) and Bert Carp (who worked for Senator Walter "Fritz" Mondale when he chaired the US Senate Select Committee on Equal Educational Opportunity).

Most important, I thank the librarians and archivists who patiently responded to my endless queries. I am indebted to Joellen El Bashir, curator at the Howard University Moorland Spingarn Research Center, Jay P. Goldman at the American Association of School Administrators, and the numerous librarians and archivists at the NAACP, Library of Congress, Maryland State Archives, Texas State Archives and Library Commission, Atlanta University Center Library, Emory University Library, and George Washington University Library. Additionally, Maura Spiegelman and Julia Merlin at the Institute for Education Statistics/National Center for Education Statistics were helpful in providing the latest national data cited in this book.

I thank a host of Howard University faculty colleagues and students for enthusiastically encouraging my work as a scholar during my deanship. I especially appreciate Dr. Richard A. English, who, as university provost, modeled being a scholar-administrator. Additionally, I thank Professor Lisa Crooms of the Howard University School of Law. Other individuals provided essential research assistance, including Russell C. Fenwick, Dr. Chike Akua, Michael B. Swygert, Dr. Carol Moye, and Sarah Spruill.

For believing in my research and asking questions that sharpened my thinking, I am forever grateful to Jayne Fargnoli, Caroline Chauncey, and Richard Milner IV. Most important, I am deeply appreciative to Faye Goolrick (who has been with me throughout this writing journey) for her expert editing of various versions of my book manuscript and the sustained imprint she has had on my writing.

Last, but not least, I want to thank those portrayed in *Jim Crow's Pink Slip*, especially the African American principals, teachers, and their allies, who, working with the NAACP and other organizations, persevered in seeking and providing a quality education for their students.

ABOUT THE AUTHOR

LESLIE T. FENWICK, PhD, is Dean Emerita of the School of Education and a professor of Education Policy at Howard University in Washington, DC. She also holds an appointment as Dean in Residence at the American Association of Colleges for Teacher Education (AACTE).

A former Visiting Fellow and Visiting Scholar at Harvard University, she has worked in every sector of American education—as a preK–12 schoolteacher and administrator in urban public and private schools; university faculty member and administrator; foundation program officer; nonprofit board member; and legislative aid in the State of Ohio Senate. In 2020, she was a candidate for US Secretary of Education.

Her widely disseminated research and opinion-editorials about education equity, leadership, and workforce diversity have appeared and been cited in the *New York Times*, *Washington Post*, and *Education Week*. She has been an invited speaker at the National Press Club and has appeared on CNN and C-SPAN discussing education equity and workforce development.

Fenwick is one of eleven members of the Scholarly Advisory Committee (SAC) for the Smithsonian National Museum of African American History and Culture—the world's third busiest museum. The SAC was established by noted historian Dr. John Hope Franklin to help set the museum's intellectual agenda and exhibition content.

She is cofounder of the Urban Superintendents Academy at the American Association of School Administrators and a consultant to CEO Action for Racial Equity founded by Tim Ryan, US Chairman and Senior Partner, PwC. Since 2017, she has held an appointment as a McDonald Character

Leadership Conference Senior Fellow at the US Military Academy at West Point, where she occasionally lectures about character leadership.

She earned a PhD in education policy at The Ohio State University, where she was a Flesher Fellow, and a BS degree in elementary education at the University of Virginia.

INDEX